PARTNERSHIP ACT 1932'- SUPREME COURT'S LEADING CASE LAWS

CASE NOTES- FACTS- FINDINGS OF APEX COURT JUDGES & CITATIONS

JAYPRAKASH BANSILAL SOMANI

All the Past & Present Judges of the Supreme Court of India.

Salute to their wisdom.

Salute to their interpretation of Law.

Salute to their elaborative judgement writing.

Supreme Court Of India.

Contents

Contents

Preface

Dear Learned Advocates ofTrial Court, High court and Supreme Court, Corporate and Individuals.

I am very delighted to provide you a book on'PARTNERSHIP ACT 1932'- SUPREME COURT'S LATEST LEADING CASE LAWs

In this book you will get...

1. Name of the Case i. e. Cause title

2.Relevant Sections discussed in the case

3. Hon'ble Judges/Coram of the case

4.Number of PDF Pages in Original Judgement of the case

5. All available Citations of the case

6. Case Note with appeal allowed/ dismissed or disposed off

7. Facts of the case

8. Hon'ble Apex Court's findings, while dismissing/allowing or disposing the appeal

9. Ratio Decidendi if any.

My special thanks to Manupatra, because of their web portal I can compile this book in well manner. I am also thankful to Notion Press to support me to publish & market this book throughout the Country. Thanks to my Juniors, Advocate Colleagues & Insolvency Professional Colleagues to support me in this venture.

Adv. Manoj Kumar Chowdhary & Miss. Pooja Rai has helped me a lot to compile this book. I hope this book will add some value addition in the wealth of your legal knowledge. Your positive feedbacks will boost me to compile/ write further books & negative feedbacks will improve my skills. Kindly send your valuable feedbacks by email.

Thanks with Regards,

Jayprakash B. Somani

Advocate, Supreme Court of India

Email: jaysomani64@gmail.com

Web Site:www.jayprakashsomani.com

Call: 9322188701, 8459194576

Acknowledgements

Printed & Published by
Notion Press
No. 8, 3rd Cross Street,
CIT Colony, Mylapore,
Chennai, Tamil Nadu- 600004
Managed by
Jayprakash Somani Advocates & Solicitors
Law Firm for Supreme Court of India
Delhi Office
B- 851, 1st Floor, Shivaji Marg, New Ashok Nagar, Delhi 110096.
Call: 9322188701, 8459194576
Supreme Court Chamber
312, 3rd Floor, M. C. Setalvad Block, In front of 'D' Gate, Bhagwan Das
Road, Supreme Court of India, New Delhi 110001
Contact: 8459194576, 9811011747
www.jayprakashsomani.com
Download our app to get access to our Free Videos, Free Bare Acts,
Free Study Material in Legal as well as International Business Regime.
Android App Link ;-https://clpandrea.page.link/cmSm
Ios APp Link :-https://apps.apple.com/us/app/classplus/id1324522260
Login with org code ;- (qywzji)
Web Link ;-https://qywzji.courses.store/
Opportunity for Lawyers/ Social Workers to get Supreme Court Law
Firm JSAS's authorised centre at District Level.
Kindly Message or Call to: 9322188701
Books are available online in India
1.**Notion Press:**https://notionpress.com/author/jayprakash_somani
2.**Amazon:**https://www.amazon.in/s?k=jayprakash+somani
3.**Flipkart:**https://www.flipkart.com/search?q=Jayprakash%20Somani
Books are available online at International Market
4. **Amazon International:** https://www.amazon.com/
s?k=jayprakash+somani
5. **Amazon United Kingdom:** https://www.amazon.co.uk/
s?k=jayprakash+somani

6. **E-Books/Kindle edition at National & International Level:** https://www.amazon.in/s?k=jaypraksh+somani

CHAPTER ONE

Sirajudheen vs. Zeenath and Ors.(27.02.2023-SC):MANU/ SC/0177/ 2023

Relative Section:

Code of Civil Procedure, 1908 (CPC) - Order XLI Rule 23, Code of Civil Procedure, 1908 (CPC) - Order XLI Rule 23A, Code of Civil Procedure, 1908 (CPC) - Order XLI Rule 24, Code of Civil Procedure, 1908 (CPC) - Order XLI Rule 27, Code of Civil Procedure, 1908 (CPC) - Order XLI Rule 27(1), Code of Civil Procedure, 1908 (CPC) - Order XLI Rule 33; Indian Evidence Act, 1872 - Section 92, Indian Evidence Act, 1872 - Section 103, Indian Evidence Act, 1872 - Section 114, Indian Evidence Act, 1872 - Section 120; Indian Partnership Act, 1932 - Section 69(1)

Hon'bleJudges/Coram:

Dinesh Maheshwari and Sudhanshu Dhulia, JJ.

Equivalent Citation:

2023(2)ALT45, 2023(2)CivilCC(S.C.), 135(2023)CLT627, 2023GLH(1)582, 2023(2)ICC400, 2023/INSC/173, 2023(2)KCCR898,2023(2) KHC577,2023(2)KLT139,(2023)2MLJ264, 2023(I)OLR922,2023(2)RCR (Civil) 55

NumberofPagesintheOriginalJudgment: 13

Case Reference:

Addanki Narayanappa and Ors. v. Bhaskara Krishtappa and Ors. MANU/ SC/0281/1966; Municipal Corporation ,Hyderabad v. Sunder Singh MANU/SC/7735/2008; A. Andisamy Chettiar v. A. Subburaj Chettiar MANU /SC/1400/2015; Pathu v. Katheesa Umma MANU/KE/0550/1990 : 1990(2) KLT SN.51; Ponnan v. Kuttipennu MANU/KE/0370/1987 : 1987 (2) KLT 455; Sanjay Kumar Singh v. State of Jharkhand MANU/SC/0305/ 2022

Case Note:

Civil - De novo trial - Maintainability of - Respondent No. 1 filed civil suit against Appellant-Defendant No. 1 and other Respondents for setting aside sale deed - Plaintiff-Respondent No. 1 also filed another civil suit for prohibitory injunction - Trial Court rejected case of Plaintiff-Respondent No. 1 with findings, that circumstances placed on record did not probabilise case that by defrauding her, husbands of her sisters got executed sale document and Sub Registrar who had registered sale deed had not been examined - In appeal, High Court directed Trial Court to decide suit afresh after dde novo trial, with observations that evidence necessary for proper determination of suit had not been brought on record - Hence, present appeal - Whether High Court erred in remanding matter for trial de novo.

Facts:

The Respondent No. 1 filed the subject civil suit against the present Appellant as Defendant No. 1 and other Respondents, her sisters, as Defendant Nos. 2 to 5, for setting aside a sale deed. Apart from the civil suit, the Plaintiff-Respondent No. 1 filed another civil suit for prohibitory injunction. After examining the evidence on record, the Trial Court rejected the case of the Plaintiff-Respondent No. 1 with the findings, inter alia the circumstances placed on record did not probabilise the case that by defrauding her, the husbands of her sisters got executed the sale document while making her believe that it were a security document for getting new films. The Trial Court also found that no steps were taken by the Plaintiff-Respondent No. 1 to examine the Sub Registrar who had registered the sale deed whereupon she had put her signatures on being allegedly made to believe it to be a security document and she failed to discharge the burden of proof. THE High Court, disposed of appeal, filed by the Plaintiff against dismissal of her suit for cancellation of a sale deed and for prohibitory injunction with directions to the Trial Court to decide the suit afresh after de novo trial, essentially with the observations that the evidence necessary for proper determination of the suit had not been brought on record.

Held, while allowing the appeal:

(i) One of the striking features of the impugned judgment was that even while dealing with a regular first appeal against the judgment and decree of the Trial Court, the High Court had not even adverted to the findings of the Trial Court pertaining to the present case and had not specified as to how the findings recorded by the Trial Court were unsustainable or unjustified. As noticed, in the impugned judgment, the High Court had narrated a few circumstances leaning in favour of the Plaintiff and then a few othercircumstances which favour the genuineness of the sale in question and thereafter, had observed that the evidence necessary for a proper determination of the suit had not been brought on record; andthat the evidence on record was insufficient to arrive at a proper finding in favour or against the sale deed in question. The High Court would further observe that material witnesses had not been examined and no evidence has been brought in with regard to passing of consideration. [11]

(ii) With respect, what turns on the observations in the impugned judgment was that the High Court was unable to arrive at a conclusion on the basis of the material on record. However, fact of the matter remains that on the basis of the same material on record, the Trial Court had indeed arrived at a definite conclusion that the Plaintiff had failed to establish her case and hence, the suit was liable to be dismissed. The High Court had not at all referred to the findings of the Trial Court and it was difficult to find from the judgment impugned as to why at all those findings of the Trial Court were not to be sustained or the decree was required to be reversed. [11.1]

(iii) For a few tentative observations about certain circumstances existing in favour of the Plaintiff and certain other circumstances existing in favour of the Defendants and then, with another observation that Plaintiff was a vital witness, the High Court was not justified in remanding the matter for trial de novo without recording any finding if the Plaintiff was prevented from examining herself or from adducing any other evidence as also without explaining as to on what ground the decree was being reversed. [15]

Disposition: Appeal Allowed

Shiv Developers vs. Aksharay Developers and Ors. (31.01.2022 - SC) : MANU/SC/0111/2022

Relative Section:

Code of Civil Procedure, 1908 (CPC) - Order VII Rule 11(d), Code of Civil Procedure, 1908 (CPC) - Order XXX Rule 1, Code of Civil Procedure, 1908 (CPC) - Order XXX Rule 2; Code of Civil Procedure, 1908 (CPC) - Section 151; Indian Partnership Act, 1932 - Section 56, Indian Partnership Act, 1932 - Section 69, Indian Partnership Act, 1932 - Section 69(1), Indian Partnership Act, 1932 - Section 69(2), Indian Partnership Act, 1932 - Section 69(3); Presidency Small Cause Courts Act, 1882 - Section 19; Presidency towns Insolvency Act, 1909; Provincial Insolvency Act, 1920; Provincial Small Cause Courts Act, 1887; Specific Relief Act, 1963; Trade Marks Act; Transfer of Property Act, 1882

Hon'bleJudges/Coram:

Dinesh Maheshwari and Vikram Nath, JJ.

Equivalent Citation: 2022(232)AIC163, AIR2022SC772, 2022(3)ALD98, 2022 (152) ALR 209, 2022(1) ALT112, (2022)2CALLT46(SC), 2022 (1) CCC 271 , 2022(3)CivilCC(S.C.), 133(2022)CLT881, 2022(2) CTC 415, 2022(3)ICC533, 2022/INSC/119, 2022(1)KLT793, (2022)2MLJ233, 2022 (2) MWN 328, 2022(89) PTC520(SC), 2022(1)RCR(Civil)802, 2022 156 RD302

NumberofPagesintheOriginalJudgment: 13

Case Reference:

Purushottam and Ors. v. Shivraj Fine Art Litho Works and Ors. MANU/ SC/8634/2006; Haldiram Bhujiawala and Ors. v. Anand Kumar Deepak Kumar and Ors. MANU/SC/0144/2000; Umesh Goel v. Himachal Pradesh Cooperative Group Housing Society Ltd. MANU/SC/0694/2016; Farooq v. Sandhya Anthraper Kurishingal and Ors. MANU/SC/0842/2017; Raptakos Brett and Co. Ltd. v. Ganesh Property MANU/SC/0595/1998

Case Note:

Civil - Declaration and injunction - Rejection of Plaint - Order VII Rule 11(d), Order 30 Rules 1 and 2 and Section 151 of the Code of Civil Procedure, 1908 read with Section 69 of the Indian Partnership Act, 1932 for rejection of plaint - Rejection sought on the ground of Suit being filed by unregistered partnership firm - Trial Court held that since suit relate to the validity of sale deed, bar of Section 69(2) would not operate - High Court reversed the finding in appeal - Hence the present appeal - Whether unregistered Partnership firm not entitled to institute suit?

Facts:

Appellant was an unregistered partnership instituted suit against Defendants. The suit emanated from purchase of subject property. According to the plaint averments, the partnership was formed exclusively for the purpose of the project related with the suit property and the tenure of the partnership was confined to the completion of the said project. Appellant had instituted the subject suit seeking perpetual injunction and declaration of the sale deed as null and void.

Held, while dismissing the Appeal:

The bar of Section 69(2) of the Act of 1932, the contract in question must be the one entered into by firm with the third-party Defendant and must also be the one entered into by the Plaintiff firm in the course of its business dealings; and that Section 69(2) of the Act of 1932 is not a bar to a suit filed by an unregistered firm, if the same is for enforcement of a statutory right or a common law right.[15]

The transaction in question was not the one entered into by the Plaintiff firm during the course of its business (i.e., of building construction); and it had been an independent transaction of sale, of the firm's share in the suit property, to the contesting Defendants. The bar of Section 69(2) is not attracted in relation to the said sale transaction. Moreover, the subject suit cannot be said to be the one for enforcement of right arising from a contract; rather the subject suit is clearly the one where the Plaintiff seeks common law remedies with the allegations of fraud and misrepresentation as also of the statutory rights of injunction and declaration in terms of the provisions of the Specific Relief Act, 1963 as also the Transfer of Property Act, 1882. Therefore, the bar of Section 69(2) of the Act of 1932 does not apply to the present case.[20]

Trial Court had rightly appreciated the facts of the case and had rightly rejected the baseless application moved by the contesting Respondents.[21]

Accordingly, this appeal allowed; the impugned judgment is set aside.[22]

Disposition: Appeal Allowed

CHAPTER THREE

Vinay Eknath Lad vs. Chiu Mao Chen (18.12.2019 - SC) : MANU /SC/1787/2019

Relative Section:

Indian Contract Act, 1872 - Section 243; Indian Evidence Act, 1872 - Section 116; Indian Partnership Act, 1932 - Section 45(1), Indian Partnership Act, 1932 - Section 48; Indian Stamp Act, 1899 - Section 36; Karnataka Stamp Act, 1957 - Section 35; Registration Act, 1908 - Section 17; Transfer Of Property Act, 1882 - Section 106, Transfer Of Property Act, 1882 - Section 109

Hon'bleJudges/Coram:

Deepak Gupta and Aniruddha Bose, JJ.

Equivalent Citation: 2021(219)AIC164, 2021 (145) ALR 757, 2020(1)ALT1, 2020(1)BLJ291, 2020(2)CivilCC(S.C.), 2019/INSC/1398, 2020-3-LW664, 2020(1)RCR(Rent)151, 2021 151 RD531, 2020 (1) SCJ 57

NumberofPagesintheOriginalJudgment: 11

Case Reference:

Bismillah Be (Dead) by L.Rs. v. Majeed Shah MANU/SC/1557/2016; Apollo Zipper India Limited v. W. Newman and Co. Ltd. MANU/SC/0431/2018; Sheela and Ors. v. Firm Prahlad Rai Prem Prakash MANU/ SC/0150/2002; Boorugu Mahadev and Sons and Ors. v. Sirigiri Narasing Rao and Ors. MANU/SC/0044/2016; S.V. Chandra Pandian and Ors. v. S.V. Sivalinga Nadar and Ors. MANU/SC/0450/1993; Dr. Chiranji Lal (D) v. Haridas MANU/SC/0396/2005 : 2005 SCC 746

Case Note:

Civil - Locus standi - Lack of - Suit was instituted claiming, inter-alia, delivery of vacant possession of subject premises and mesne profit - Original Plaintiffs claim to have had derived their right, title and interest to subject premises from partnership firm after its dissolution - Trial Court decreed suit for possession as well as mesne profit from date of service of notice of termination - Defendant, however, was successful in his appeal before High Court and judgment of Trial Court was reversed - High Court accepted Defendant's stand that Plaintiffs could not establish their locus standi to institute suit for recovery of possession - Hence, present appeal - Whether original Plaintiffs had locus to institute suit.

Facts:

The suit was instituted claiming, inter-alia, delivery of vacant possession of the subject premises and mesne profit. The original Plaintiffs claim to have had derived their right, title and interest to the subject premises from the partnership firm after its dissolution. The Trial Court decreed the suit for possession as well as mesne profit from the date of service of notice of termination. The Defendant, however, was successful in his appeal before the High Court and the judgment of the Trial Court was reversed.

Held, while allowing the appeal:

(i) The plaint, exhibits and deposition of the Plaintiffs' witness do not adequately explain the journey of the subject premises from the erstwhile partnership firm, which had inducted mother of the present Defendant as a tenant, to the seventeen individuals operating as a co-ownership firm. [14]

(ii) Without the aid of documents annexed to the interlocutory application, the Trial Court found Plaintiffs had established title superior to that of the tenant in respect of the subject premises. The Trial Court had proceeded on a principle akin to admission by the Defendant of Plaintiffs' position as that of the landlords of the subject-premises. That was the underlying reasoning of the Trial Court's judgment. According to the original Plaintiffs, the Defendant entered into negotiation with them. The said notice, however, was not made exhibit. The High Court, in the judgment under appeal had not dealt with finding of the Trial Court on this aspect of the suit. This was a point which could have material impact on adjudication of the rival claims. This Court hold so because the Defendant's defence on derivative title would not survive if the Appellant could establish that from the notice the ownership of seventeen original Plaintiffs could be established. In that event, Section 116 of the Evidence Act, 1872 would become applicable. The Defendant's continued payment of rent thereafter would constitute acknowledging the said Plaintiffs as his landlord. This would result in creation of attornment, as held in the cases of Bismilla Be and Apollo Zippers. To conclude this part of the controversy, factual enquiry was necessary which the High Court exercising its appellate jurisdiction had not gone into. [18]

(iii) Sufficient material was not there before the first two Courts to establish the original Plaintiffs' claim of ownership of the subject premises on the basis of a family arrangement after dissolution of the firm. The Appellant's attempt to adduce additional documents to establish his stand on that point had been rejected at this stage. The ratio of the judgment in the case of S.V. Chandra Pandian could not be applied in the present proceeding as there was no material to conclude that the original Plaintiffs' title to the subject-premises came from residue assets of the dissolved firm. In a landlord-tenant suit, the landlord was not required to prove his title in the subject property as in a title-suit. But when the landlord's derivative title was challenged, the same had to be established in some form. On this point the original Plaintiffs had failed before the first two Courts. [19]

(iv) Therefore, set aside the judgment under appeal and remand the matter to the High Court for readjudicating the rival claims and defence. [20]

Disposition: Appeal Allowed.

CHAPTER FOUR

P. Mohanraj and Ors. vs. Shah Brothers Ispat Pvt. Ltd. (01.03.2021 - SC) : MANU/ SC/0132/2021

Relative Section:

Arbitration Act, 1940 - Section 8(2); Arbitration And Conciliation Act, 1996 - Section 34; Bihar Reorganisation Act, 2000 - Section 89, Bihar Reorganisation Act, 2000 - Section 89(3); Bombay Relief Undertakings (special Provisions) Act, 1958 - Section 2(2), Bombay Relief Undertakings (special Provisions) Act, 1958 - Section 3, Bombay Relief Undertakings (special Provisions) Act, 1958 - Section 4(1); Code of Criminal Procedure (CrPC), 1861; Code of Civil Procedure, 1908 (CPC) - Order 21 Rule 58, Code of Civil Procedure, 1908 (CPC) - Section 26; Code of Criminal Procedure, 1898 (CrPC); Code of Criminal Procedure, 1973 (CrPC) - Section 2(d), Code of Criminal Procedure, 1973 (CrPC) - Section 4(2), Code of Criminal Procedure, 1973 (CrPC) - Section 6, Code of Criminal Procedure, 1973 (CrPC) - Section 29(2), Code of Criminal Procedure, 1973 (CrPC) - Section 62, Code of Criminal Procedure, 1973 (CrPC) - Section 63, Code of Criminal Procedure, 1973 (CrPC) - Section 64, Code of Criminal Procedure, 1973 (CrPC) - Section 82, Code of Criminal Procedure, 1973 (CrPC) - Section 173, Code of Criminal Procedure, 1973 (CrPC) - Section 177, Code of Criminal Procedure, 1973 (CrPC) - Section 178, Code of Criminal Procedure, 1973 (CrPC) - Section 179, Code of Criminal Procedure, 1973 (CrPC) - Section 180, Code of Criminal Procedure, 1973 (CrPC) - Section 181, Code of Criminal Procedure, 1973 (CrPC) - Section

182, Code of Criminal Procedure, 1973 (CrPC) - Section 183, Code of Criminal Procedure, 1973 (CrPC) - Section 184, Code of Criminal Procedure, 1973 (CrPC) - Section 185, Code of Criminal Procedure, 1973 (CrPC) - Section 186, Code of Criminal Procedure, 1973 (CrPC) - Section 187, Code of Criminal Procedure, 1973 (CrPC) - Section 188, Code of Criminal Procedure, 1973 (CrPC) - Section 189, Code of Criminal Procedure, 1973 (CrPC) - Section 258, Code of Criminal Procedure, 1973 (CrPC) - Section 264, Code of Criminal Procedure, 1973 (CrPC) - Section 320, Code of Criminal Procedure, 1973 (CrPC) - Section 320(1), Code of Criminal Procedure, 1973 (CrPC) - Section 320(2), Code of Criminal Procedure, 1973 (CrPC) - Section 320(9), Code of Criminal Procedure, 1973 (CrPC) - Section 345, Code of Criminal Procedure, 1973 (CrPC) - Section 357, Code of Criminal Procedure, 1973 (CrPC) - Section 357(1), Code of Criminal Procedure, 1973 (CrPC) - Section 357(3), Code of Criminal Procedure, 1973 (CrPC) - Section 421, Code of Criminal Procedure, 1973 (CrPC) - Section 431, Code of Criminal Procedure, 1973 (CrPC) - Section 482; Code of Criminal Procedure, 1974 (CrPC); Companies Act, 1956 - Section 391, Companies Act, 1956 - Section 442, Companies Act, 1956 - Section 446, Companies Act, 1956 - Section 446(1), Companies Act, 1956 - Section 446(2), Companies Act, 1956 - Section 454(5), Companies Act, 1956 - Section 454(5A), Companies Act, 1956 - Section 457, Companies Act, 1956 - Section 630, Companies Act, 1956 - Section 630(1); Companies Act, 2013 - Section 2; Companies (Amendment) Act, 1960; Constitution of India - Article 12, Constitution of India - Article 19, Constitution of India - Article 19(1), Constitution of India - Article 19(2), Constitution of India - Article 32, Constitution of India - Article 132, Constitution of India - Article 133, Constitution of India - Article 133(1), Constitution of India - Article 136, Constitution of India - Article 226, Constitution of India - Article 233, Constitution of India - Article 234, Constitution of India - Article 235; Contempt of Courts Act, 1952; Contempt Of Courts Act, 1971 - Section 2(b), Contempt Of Courts Act, 1971 - Section 11, Contempt Of Courts Act, 1971 - Section 12, Contempt Of Courts Act, 1971 - Section 12(1), Contempt Of Courts Act, 1971 - Section 12(4), Contempt Of Courts Act, 1971 - Section 12(5), Contempt Of Courts Act, 1971 - Section 14, Contempt Of Courts Act, 1971 - Section 15, Contempt Of Courts Act, 1971 - Section 17, Contempt Of Courts Act, 1971 - Section 23; Employees' Provident Funds And Miscellaneous Provisions Act, 1952 - Section 2(e); English And Foreign Languages

University Act, 2006 - Section 45(2); Indian Partnership Act, 1932 - Section 69(3); Indian Penal Code, 1860 (IPC) - Section 53, Indian Penal Code, 1860 (IPC) - Section 64, Indian Penal Code, 1860 (IPC) - Section 214, Indian Penal Code, 1860 (IPC) - Section 364A; Industrial Disputes Act, 1947 - Section 2(j); Insolvency And Bankruptcy Code, 2016 - Section 3(18), Insolvency And Bankruptcy Code, 2016 - Section 3(33), Insolvency And Bankruptcy Code, 2016 - Section 5(8), Insolvency And Bankruptcy Code, 2016 - Section 7, Insolvency And Bankruptcy Code, 2016 - Section 8, Insolvency And Bankruptcy Code, 2016 - Section 9, Insolvency And Bankruptcy Code, 2016 - Section 14, Insolvency And Bankruptcy Code, 2016 - Section 14(1), Insolvency And Bankruptcy Code, 2016 - Section 14(2), Insolvency And Bankruptcy Code, 2016 - Section 14(3), Insolvency And Bankruptcy Code, 2016 - Section 14(4), Insolvency And Bankruptcy Code, 2016 - Section 17, Insolvency And Bankruptcy Code, 2016 - Section 25(1), Insolvency And Bankruptcy Code, 2016 - Section 25, Insolvency And Bankruptcy Code, 2016 - Section 25(2), Insolvency And Bankruptcy Code, 2016 - Section 29A, Insolvency And Bankruptcy Code, 2016 - Section 31, Insolvency And Bankruptcy Code, 2016 - Section 31(1), Insolvency And Bankruptcy Code, 2016 - Section 32, Insolvency And Bankruptcy Code, 2016 - Section 32A, Insolvency And Bankruptcy Code, 2016 - Section 32A(1), Insolvency And Bankruptcy Code, 2016 - Section 33, Insolvency And Bankruptcy Code, 2016 - Section 33(5), Insolvency And Bankruptcy Code, 2016 - Section 35, Insolvency And Bankruptcy Code, 2016 - Section 35(1), Insolvency And Bankruptcy Code, 2016 - Section 52, Insolvency And Bankruptcy Code, 2016 - Section 80, Insolvency And Bankruptcy Code, 2016 - Section 81, Insolvency And Bankruptcy Code, 2016 - Section 81(3), Insolvency And Bankruptcy Code, 2016 - Section 84, Insolvency And Bankruptcy Code, 2016 - Section 85, Insolvency And Bankruptcy Code, 2016 - Section 86, Insolvency And Bankruptcy Code, 2016 - Section 91(2), Insolvency And Bankruptcy Code, 2016 - Section 94, Insolvency And Bankruptcy Code, 2016 - Section 95, Insolvency And Bankruptcy Code, 2016 - Section 96, Insolvency And Bankruptcy Code, 2016 - Section 96(1), Insolvency And Bankruptcy Code, 2016 - Section 96(3), Insolvency And Bankruptcy Code, 2016 - Section 100, Insolvency And Bankruptcy Code, 2016 - Section 101, Insolvency And Bankruptcy Code, 2016 - Section 101(1), Insolvency And Bankruptcy Code, 2016 - Section 101(3), Insolvency And Bankruptcy Code, 2016 - Section 114; Limited Liability Partnership Act 2008 - Section 2; Negotiable Instruments Act, 1881 -

Section 138, Negotiable Instruments Act, 1881 - Section 139, Negotiable Instruments Act, 1881 - Section 140, Negotiable Instruments Act, 1881 - Section 141, Negotiable Instruments Act, 1881 - Section 141(1), Negotiable Instruments Act, 1881 - Section 142, Negotiable Instruments Act, 1881 - Section 142(1), Negotiable Instruments Act, 1881 - Section 142(2), Negotiable Instruments Act, 1881 - Section 143, Negotiable Instruments Act, 1881 - Section 143A, Negotiable Instruments Act, 1881 - Section 143A(1), Negotiable Instruments Act, 1881 - Section 144, Negotiable Instruments Act, 1881 - Section 145, Negotiable Instruments Act, 1881 - Section 146, Negotiable Instruments Act, 1881 - Section 147, Negotiable Instruments Act, 1881 - Section 148, Negotiable Instruments Act, 1881 - Section 148(1), Negotiable Instruments Act, 1881 - Section 149, Negotiable Instruments Act, 1881 - Section 150, Negotiable Instruments Act, 1881 - Section 151, Negotiable Instruments Act, 1881 - Section 152, Negotiable Instruments Act, 1881 - Section 153; Prevention Of Money-laundering Act, 2002 - Section 14(1); Sick Industrial Companies (special Provisions) Act, 1985 - Section 22, Sick Industrial Companies (special Provisions) Act, 1985 - Section 22(1); State Financial Corporations Act, 1951 - Section 29, State Financial Corporations Act, 1951 - Section 31; Insolvency and Bankruptcy Code (Amendment) Act, 2020; Securitisation and Reconstruction of Financial Assets and Enforcement of Security Interest Act, 2002; Prevention of Corruption Act, 1988; Banking, Public Financial Institutions and Negotiable Instruments Laws (Amendment) Act, 1988; Negotiable Instruments (Amendment and Miscellaneous Provisions) Act, 2002; General Clauses Act, 1897; Evidence Act; Income-Tax Act, 1961; Indian Companies Act

Hon'bleJudges/Coram:
Rohinton Fali Nariman, Navin Sinha and K.M. Joseph, JJ.

Equivalent Citation: Civil Appeal No. 10355 of 2018, Criminal Appeal No. 239 of 2021 (Arising out of Special Leave Petition (Crl.) No. 1955 of 2021) (Diary No. 32585/2019), Criminal Appeal No. 240 of 2021 (Arising out of Special Leave Petition (Crl.) No. 10587 of 2019), Criminal Appeal No. 241 of 2021 (Arising out of Special Leave Petition (Crl.) No. 10857 of 2019), Criminal Appeal No. 242 of 2021 (Arising out of Special Leave Petition (Crl.) No. 10550 of 2019), Criminal Appeal No. 243 of 2021 (Arising out of Special Leave Petition (Crl.) No. 10858 of 2019), Criminal Appeal No. 244 of 2021 (Arising out of Special Leave Petition (Crl.) No. 10860 of 2019), Criminal Appeal No. 245 of 2021 (Arising out of Special

Leave Petition (Crl.) No. 10861 of 2019), Criminal Appeal No. 246 of 2021 (Arising out of Special Leave Petition (Crl.) No. 10446 of 2019), Criminal Appeal Nos. 247-248 of 2021 (Arising out of Special Leave Petition (Crl.) Nos. 2246-2247 of 2020), Criminal Appeal No. 200 of 2021 (Arising out of Special Leave Petition (Crl.) No. 2496 of 2020), Criminal Appeal No. 199 of 2021 (Arising out of Special Leave Petition (Crl.) No. 3500 of 2020), Writ Petition (Criminal) Nos. 330, 339 of 2020, Writ Petition (Civil) No. 982 of 2020, Writ Petition (Criminal) Nos. 297, 342 of 2020, Criminal Appeal Nos. 201-204 of 2021 (Arising out of Special Leave Petition (Crl.) Nos. 5638-5651 of 2020), Criminal Appeal Nos. 215-230 of 2021 (Arising out of Special Leave Petition (Crl.) Nos. 5653-5668 of 2020), Writ Petition (Civil) Nos. 1417, 1439 of 2020, 18 of 2021, Writ Petition (Criminal) Nos. 9 and 26 of 2021

NumberofPagesintheOriginalJudgment: 39

Case Reference:

Aneeta Hada and Ors. v. Godfather Travels and Tours Pvt. Ltd. and Ors. MANU/SC/0335/2012; State of Assam v. Ranga Mahammad and Ors. MANU/SC/0056/1966; Jagdish Chander Gupta v. Kajaria Traders (India) Ltd. MANU/SC/0047/1964; Rajasthan State Electricity Board, Jaipur v. Mohan Lal and Ors. MANU/SC/0360/1967; C.B.I., Patna and Ors. v. Braj Bhushan Prasad and Ors. MANU/SC/0614/2001; Bangalore Water Supply and Sewerage Board v. A. Rajappa and Ors. MANU/SC/0257/1978; Rohit Pulp and Paper Mills Ltd. v. Collector of Central Excise, Baroda MANU/SC/0186/1991; Oswal Agro Mills Ltd. and Ors. v. Collector of Central Excise and Ors. MANU/SC/0344/1993; K. Bhagirathi G. Shenoy and Ors. v. K.P. Ballakuraya and Ors. MANU/SC/0236/1999; Lokmat Newspapers Pvt. Ltd. v. Shankarprasad MANU/SC/0405/1999; Godfrey Phillips India Ltd. and Ors. v. State of U.P. and Ors. MANU/SC/0051/2005; Rainbow Steels Ltd., Muzaffarnagar and Ors. v. C.S.T., U.P. and Ors. MANU/SC/0408/1981; The State of Bombay and Ors. v. The Hospital Mazdoor Sabha and Ors. MANU/SC/0200/1960; Vikram Singh and Ors. v. Union of India (UOI) and Ors. MANU/SC/0901/2015; Siddeshwari Cotton Mills (P) Ltd. v. Union of India (UOI) and Ors. MANU/SC/0359/1989; Tribhuban Parkash Nayyar v. The Union of India (UOI) MANU/SC/0029/1969; The U.P. State Electricity Board and Ors. v. Hari Shankar Jain and Ors. MANU/SC/0500/1978; Grasim Industries Ltd. v. Collector of Customs, Bombay MANU/SC/0256/2002; Pioneer Urban Land and Infrastructure Limited and Ors. v. Union of India (UOI) and Ors. MANU/SC/1071/2019; Controller of Estate Duty,

Gujarat and Ors. v. Kantilal Trikamlal and Ors. MANU/SC/0520/1976; Subramanian Swamy v. Union of India (UOI) and Ors. MANU/SC/0621/ 2016; R.L. Arora v. State of Uttar Pradesh and Ors. MANU/SC/0033/1964; Ahmedabad Pvt. Primary Teachers' Association v. Administrative Officer and Ors. MANU/SC/0032/2004; Swiss Ribbons Pvt. Ltd. and Ors. v. Union of India (UOI) and Ors. MANU/SC/0079/2019; Macquarie Bank Limited v. Shilpi Cable Technologies Ltd. MANU/SC/1609/2017; Giriraj Garg v. Coal India Ltd. and Ors. MANU/SC/0212/2019; Goaplast Pvt. Ltd. v. Chico Ursula D'Souza and Ors. MANU/SC/0200/2003; Vinay Devanna Nayak v. Ryot Seva Sahakari Bank Ltd. MANU/SC/0061/2008; Electronics Trade and Technology Development Corpn. Ltd., Secunderabad v. Indian Technologists and Engineers (Electronics) Pvt. Ltd. and Ors. MANU/SC/ 0591/1996; Damodar S. Prabhu v. Sayed Babalal H. MANU/SC/0319/2010; K.M. Ibrahim v. K.P. Mohammed and Ors. MANU/SC/1865/2009; JIK Industries Limited and Ors. v. Amarlal V. Jumani and Ors. MANU/SC/ 0075/2012; Kaushalya Devi Massand v. Roopkishore Khore MANU/SC/ 0385/2011; R. Vijayan v. Baby and Ors. MANU/SC/1245/2011; Dashrath Rupsingh Rathod v. State of Maharashtra MANU/SC/0655/2014; Frick India Ltd. v. Union of India (UOI) and Ors. MANU/SC/0787/1989; Forage and Co. (of Lushala) v. Municipal Corpn. of Greater Bombay and Ors. MANU/SC/0709/1999; Lafarge Aggregates and Concrete India P. Ltd. v. Sukarsh Azad and Ors. MANU/SC/1183/2013; Rajneesh Aggarwal v. Amit J. Bhalla MANU/SC/1462/2001; Meters and Instruments Private Limited and Ors. v. Kanchan Mehta MANU/SC/1256/2017; Goa Plast (P) Ltd. v. Chico Ursula D'Souza MANU/SC/0940/2003; Rangappa v. Mohan MANU/ SC/0376/2010; M. Abbas Haji v. T.N. Channakeshava MANU/SC/1302/ 2019; Zahira Habibulla H. Sheikh and Ors. v. State of Gujarat and Ors. MANU/SC/0322/2004; Abhilash Vinodkumar Jain v. Cox and Kings (India) Ltd. and Ors. MANU/SC/0303/1995; Dulal Chandra Bhar and Ors. v. Sukumar Banerjee and Ors. MANU/WB/0120/1958; Niaz Mohammad and Ors. v. State of Haryana and Ors. MANU/SC/0063/1995; T.N. Godavarman Thirumulpad through the Amicus Curiae v. Ashok Khot and Ors. MANU/SC/2520/2006; Sahdeo v. State of U.P. and Ors. MANU/SC/ 0132/2010; B.K. Kar v. The Chief Justice and His Companion Judges of The High Court of Orissa and Ors. MANU/SC/0111/1961; Sukhdev Singh Sodhi v. The Hon'ble Chief Justice S. Teja Singh and Ors. MANU/SC/0134/ 1953; S. Abdul Karim and Ors. v. M.K. Prakash and Ors. MANU/SC/0165/ 1976; Chhotu Ram v. Urvashi Gulati and Ors. MANU/SC/0492/2001; Anil

Ratan Sarkar and Ors. v. Hirak Ghosh and Ors. MANU/SC/0175/2002; Daroga Singh and Ors. v. B.K. Pandey MANU/SC/0336/2004; All India Anna Dravida Munnetra Kazhagam v. L.K. Tripathi and Ors. MANU/SC/0509/2009; Mrityunjoy Das and Ors. v. Sayed Hasibur Rahaman and Ors. MANU/SC/0177/2001; V.G. Nigam and Ors. v. Kedar Nath Gupta and Ors. MANU/SC/0419/1992; Murray and Co. v. Ashok Kr. Newatia and Ors. MANU/SC/0042/2000; Maninderjit Singh Bitta v. Union of India (UOI) and Ors. MANU/SC/1246/2011; Kanwar Singh Saini v. High Court of Delhi MANU/SC/1111/2011; T.C. Gupta v. Bimal Kumar Dutta and Ors. MANU/SC/1102/2013; BSI Ltd. and Ors. v. Gift Holdings Pvt. Ltd. and Ors. MANU/SC/2443/2000; Maharashtra Tubes Ltd. v. State Industrial and Investment Corporation of Maharashtra Ltd. and Ors. MANU/SC/0427/1993; Kusum Ingots and Alloys Ltd. and Ors. v. Pennar Peterson Securities Ltd. and Ors. MANU/SC/0127/2000; S.V. Kondaskar v. V.M. Deshpande and Ors. MANU/SC/0336/1972; Sudarsan Chits (I) Ltd. v. O. Sukumaran Pillai and Ors. MANU/SC/0037/1984; Central Bank of India v. Elmot Engineering Co. and Ors. MANU/SC/0485/1994; Inderjit C. Parekh and Ors. v. V.K. Bhatt and Ors. MANU/SC/0368/1974; Sheoratan Agarwal and Ors. v. State of Madhya Pradesh MANU/SC/0112/1984; State of Madras v. C.V. Parekh and Ors. MANU/SC/0195/1970; Anil Hada v. Indian Acrylic Limited MANU/SC/0736/1999; U.P. Pollution Control Board v. Modi Distillery and Ors. MANU/SC/0912/1987; State Bank of India v. V. Ramakrishnan MANU/SC/0849/2018 : (2018) 17 SCC 394; Magnhild v. McIntyre Bros. & Co. (1920) 3 KB 321; Allen v. Emerson 1944 IKB 362 : (1944) 1 All ER 344; Hood-Barrs v. IRC (1946) 2 All ER 768 (CA); United Towns Electric Co. Ltd. v. Attorney General for Newfoundland (1939) 1 All ER 423 (PC); Tillmanns and Co. v. S.S. Knutsford Ltd. MANU/MT/0003/1908 : (1908) 2 KB 385 (CA); Attorney General v. Leicester Corporation (1910) 2 Ch 359: (1908-10) All ER Rep Ext 1002; National Assn. of Local Govt. Officers v. Bolton Corpn. 1943 AC 166 : (1942) 2 All ER 425 (HL); Bank of India v. Vijay Transport 1988 Supp SCC 47; Manish Kumar v. Union of India; CIT v. Ishwarlal Bhagwandas (1966) 1 SCR 190; Legal Remembrancer v. Matilal Ghose MANU/WB/0026/1913 : I.L.R. 41 Cal. 173; Andre Paul Terence Ambard v. Attorney-General of Trinidad and Tobago MANU/PR/0109/1936 : AIR 1936 PC 141; D.K. Kapur v. Reserve Bank of India MANU/DE/0038/2001 : (2001) 58 DRJ 424 (DB); Indorama Synthetics (I) Ltd. v. State of Maharashtra MANU/MH/0692/2016 : (2016) 4 Mah LJ 249; Power Grid Corporation of India Ltd. v. Jyoti Structures Ltd. MANU/DE/5162/2017 :

(2018) 246 DLT 485; Deputy Director, Directorate of Enforcement Delhi v. Axis Bank MANU/DE/1120/2019 : (2019) 259 DLT 500; Tayal Cotton Pvt. Ltd. v. State of Maharashtra MANU/MH/2352/2018 : (2019) 1 Mah LJ 312; MBL Infrastructure Ltd. v. Manik Chand Somani CRR 3456/2018; Makwana Mangaldas Tulsidas v. State of Gujarat MANU/SC/0517/2020; M. v. Home Office (1993) 3 All ER 537 : (1994) 1 AC 377 : (1993) 3 WLR 433 (HL); H.N. Jagadeesh v. R. Rajeshwari MANU/SCOR/84514/2017

Case Note:

Insolvency -Criminal Proceedings - Moratorium - Scope - Sections 138 and 141 of the Negotiable Instruments Act, 1881 (NI Act) - Section 14 of the Insolvency and Bankruptcy Code, 2016 (IBC) - Cheques issues dishonoured - Criminal complaints initiated followed by proceedings under IBC - Whether proceedings under Section 138 and 141 of the NI Act covered by the moratorium provision under the IBC?

Facts:

The issue involved in the instant case pertains scope of Section 14 of the Insolvency and Bankruptcy Code, 2016 (IBC) vis-Ã-vis proceedings under Sections 138/141 of the Negotiable Instruments Act, 1881 (NI Act). The issue brought up for adjudication was whether criminal proceedings under NI Act would be covered within the scope of moratorium as provided for in IBC. In the present case, several cheques issued in favour of the Respondent were returned dishonoured by reason of insufficient funds. While proceedings were initiated under NI Act, a statutory notice under Section 8 of the IBC was issued by the Respondent to the Company and the Respondent filed a Section 9 petition before the National Company Law Tribunal ('NCLT'). The application was admitted and corporate insolvency resolution process directed to be commenced and moratorium was declared. Thereafter, proceedings in two criminal complaints were stayed. NCLAT set aside the order while holding that Section 138 being a criminal law provision, not a 'proceeding' within the meaning of Section 14 of the IBC. Thereafter, resolution plan was approved as a result of which the moratorium order ceased to have effect. Hence, the present proceedings.

Held, while allowing the Appeals:

A cursory look at Section 14(1) makes it clear that subject to the exceptions contained in Sub-sections (2) and (3), on the insolvency commencement date, the Adjudicating Authority shall mandatorily, by order, declare a moratorium to prohibit what follows in Clauses (a) to (d). Importantly, Under Sub-section (4), this order of moratorium does not continue indefinitely, but has effect only from the date of the order declaring moratorium till the completion of the corporate insolvency resolution process which is time bound, either culminating in the order of the Adjudicating Authority approving a resolution plan or in liquidation. [10]

It can thus be seen that regard being had to the object sought to be achieved by the IBC in imposing this moratorium, a quasi-criminal proceeding which would result in the assets of the corporate debtor being depleted as a result of having to pay compensation which can amount to twice the amount of the cheque that has bounced would directly impact the corporate insolvency resolution process in the same manner as the institution, continuation, or execution of a decree in such suit in a civil court for the amount of debt or other liability. Judged from the point of view of this objective, it is impossible to discern any difference between the impact of a suit and a Section 138 proceeding, insofar as the corporate debtor is concerned, on its getting the necessary breathing space to get back on its feet during the corporate insolvency resolution process. Given this fact, it is difficult to accept that noscitur a sociis or ejusdem generis should be used to cut down the width of the expression "proceedings" so as to make such proceedings analogous to civil suits. [24]

Viewed from another point of view, Clause (b) of Section 14(1) also makes it clear that during the moratorium period, any transfer, encumbrance, alienation, or disposal by the corporate debtor of any of its assets or any legal right or beneficial interest therein being also interdicted, yet a liability in the form of compensation payable Under Section 138 would somehow escape the dragnet of Section 14(1). While Section 14(1)(a) refers to monetary liabilities of the corporate debtor, Section 14(1)(b) refers to the corporate debtor's assets, and together, these two clauses form a scheme which shields the corporate debtor from pecuniary attacks against it in the moratorium period so that the corporate debtor gets breathing space to continue as a going concern in order to ultimately rehabilitate itself. Any crack in this shield is bound to have adverse consequences, given the object of Section 14, and cannot, by any process of interpretation, be allowed to occur. [25]

Since the corporate debtor would be covered by the moratorium provision contained in Section 14 of the IBC, by which continuation of Section 138/141 proceedings against the corporate debtor and initiation of Section 138/141 proceedings against the said debtor during the corporate insolvency resolution process are interdicted. The legal impediment contained in Section 14 of the IBC would make it impossible for such proceeding to continue or be instituted against the corporate debtor. Thus, for the period of moratorium, since no Section 138/141 proceeding can continue or be initiated against the corporate debtor because of a statutory bar, such proceedings can be initiated or continued against the persons mentioned in Section 141(1) and (2) of the Negotiable Instruments Act. This being the case, it is clear that the moratorium provision contained in Section 14 of the IBC would apply only to the corporate debtor, the natural persons mentioned in Section 141 continuing to be statutorily liable under Chapter XVII of the Negotiable Instruments Act[77]

A Section 138/141 proceeding against a corporate debtor is covered by Section 14(1)(a) of the IBC.[78]

Resultantly, the civil appeal is allowed and the judgment under appeal is set aside. [79]

Ratio Decidendi: Proceedings of cheque dishonour under Sections 138/ 141 of the Negotiable Instruments Act against a corporate debtor covered by Section 14(1)(a) of the Insolvency and Bankruptcy Code

Disposition: Appeal Allowed.

CHAPTER FIVE

Umesh Goel vs. Himachal Pradesh Cooperative Group Housing Society Ltd. (29.06.2016 – SC) : MANU/ SC/0694/2016

Relative Section:

Indian Partnership Act, 1932 - Section 2, Indian Partnership Act, 1932 - Section 56, Indian Partnership Act, 1932 - Section 69, Indian Partnership Act, 1932 - Section 69(1), Indian Partnership Act, 1932 - Section 69(2), Indian Partnership Act, 1932 - Section 69(3), Indian Partnership Act, 1932 - Section 69(4); Arbitration and Conciliation Act, 1996 - Section 2(1), Arbitration and Conciliation Act, 1996 - Section 9, Arbitration and Conciliation Act, 1996 - Section 11(5), Arbitration and Conciliation Act, 1996 - Section 34, Arbitration and Conciliation Act, 1996 - Section 35, Arbitration and Conciliation Act, 1996 - Section 36, Arbitration and Conciliation Act, 1996 - Section 37; Limitation Act, 1963 - Section 14; Interest Act, 1978 - Section 2; Code of Civil Procedure, 1908 (CPC);Presidency-Towns Insolvency Act, 1909;Provincial Insolvency Act, 1920;Presidency Small Cause Courts Act, 1882 - Section 19; Provincial Small Cause Courts Act, 1887;Indian Contract Act, 1872;Arbitration Act, 1940 [Repealed] - Section 2, Arbitration Act, 1940 [Repealed] - Section 8, Arbitration Act, 1940 [Repealed] - Section 8(1), Arbitration Act, 1940 [Repealed] - Section 8(2), Arbitration Act, 1940 [Repealed] - Section 9,

Arbitration Act, 1940 [Repealed] - Section 11, Arbitration Act, 1940 [Repealed] - Section 12, Arbitration Act, 1940 [Repealed] - Section 14, Arbitration Act, 1940 [Repealed] - Section 15, Arbitration Act, 1940 [Repealed] - Section 16, Arbitration Act, 1940 [Repealed] - Section 17, Arbitration Act, 1940 [Repealed] - Section 18, Arbitration Act, 1940 [Repealed] - Section 19, Arbitration Act, 1940 [Repealed] - Section 20, Arbitration Act, 1940 [Repealed] - Section 21, Arbitration Act, 1940 [Repealed] - Section 23, Arbitration Act, 1940 [Repealed] - Section 24, Arbitration Act, 1940 [Repealed] - Section 25, Arbitration Act, 1940 [Repealed] - Section 27, Arbitration Act, 1940 [Repealed] - Section 28, Arbitration Act, 1940 [Repealed] - Section 29, Arbitration Act, 1940 [Repealed] - Section 30, Arbitration Act, 1940 [Repealed] - Section 31, Arbitration Act, 1940 [Repealed] - Section 32, Arbitration Act, 1940 [Repealed] - Section 33, Arbitration Act, 1940 [Repealed] - Section 34, Arbitration Act, 1940 [Repealed] - Section 36, Arbitration Act, 1940 [Repealed] - Section 37, Arbitration Act, 1940 [Repealed] - Section 38, Arbitration Act, 1940 [Repealed] - Section 39, Arbitration Act, 1940 [Repealed] - Section 40, Arbitration Act, 1940 [Repealed] - Section 41, Arbitration Act, 1940 [Repealed] - Section 42, Arbitration Act, 1940 [Repealed] - Section 43, Arbitration Act, 1940 [Repealed] - Section 47, Arbitration Act, 1940 [Repealed] - Section 48, Arbitration Act, 1940 [Repealed] - Section 49, Arbitration Act, 1940 [Repealed] - Section 50, Arbitration Act, 1940 [Repealed] - Section 56, Arbitration Act, 1940 [Repealed] - Section 58, Arbitration Act, 1940 [Repealed] - Section 59

Hon'bleJudges/Coram:

F.M. Ibrahim Kalifulla and C. Nagappan, JJ.

Equivalent Citation: 2016(164)AIC224, AIR2016SC3116, 2016(5)ALD57, 2016(6)ALLMR918, 2016 (117) ALR 709, 2016(4)ARBLR96(SC), 2016 5 AWC4479SC, 2016(5)BomCR112, (2017)1CALLT75(SC), 2016 (3) CCC 122 , 2016(3)CDR696(SC), 2016(4) CHN (SC) 75, [2016]134CLA164(SC), 122(2016)CLT682, 2016(4)CTC419, 2016(II)CLR(SC)253, 2016/INSC/457, 2016 (3) KHC 881, 2016(3)KLT228, (2016) 5ML J587,2016(II)OLR431, 2016(4)RCR(Civil)54, 2017(1)RLW16(SC),2016(5)SCALE844,(2016)11SCC313, 2016 (7) SCJ 549, [2016]137SCL1(SC), [2016]6SCR703

NumberofPagesintheOriginalJudgment:16

Case Reference:

Jagdish Chander Gupta v. Kajaria Traders (India) Ltd. MANU/SC/0047/ 1964 : 1964 (8) SCR 50 : AIR 1964 SC 1882; Kamal Pushp Enterprises v. D.R. Construction Co. MANU/SC/0465/2000 : (2000) 6 SCC 659; The Bharat Bank, Ltd., Delhi v. The Employees of the Bharat Bank Ltd., Delhi and the Bharat Bank Employees' Union, Delhi MANU/SC/0030/1950 : AIR 1950 SC 188; Firm Ashok Traders and Anr. v. Gurumukh Das Saluja and Ors. MANU/SC/0026/2004 : (2004) 3 SCC 155; Sumtibai and Ors. v. Paras Finance Co. Regd. Partnership Firm, Beawer (Raj.) Through Mankanwar (Smt.) W/o Parasmal Chordia (Dead) and Ors. MANU/SC/7987/2007 : (2007) 10 SCC 82; Panchu Gopal Bose v. Board of Trustees for Port of Calcutta MANU/SC/0385/1994 : (1993) 4 SCC 338; Consolidated Engg. Enterprises v. Principal Secy. Irrigation Deptt. and Ors. MANU/SC/7460/ 2008 : 2008 (6) SCALE 748; State of W.B. v. Sadan K. Bormal and Anr. MANU/SC/0441/2004 : (2004) 6 SCC 59; Raj Kumar Khurana v. State of (NCT of Delhi) and Anr. MANU/SC/0727/2009 : (2009) 6 SCC 72; Indian Oil Corporation Limited Rep. by Its Chief LPG Manager (Engg.) S. Chandran v. Devi Constructions, Engineering Contractors and Anr. MANU/ DE/2724/2009 : 2009 (2) Law Weekly 849; Delhi Development Authority v. Kochhar Construction Work and Anr. MANU/SC/1279/1998 : (1998) 8 SCC 559; P. Sarathy v. State Bank of India MANU/SC/0422/2000 : (2000) 5 SCC 355; East End Dwelling Co. Ltd. v. Finsbury Borough Council (1951) 2 ALL ER 587; Paramjeet Singh Patheja v. ICDS Ltd. MANU/SC/4798/2006 : (2006) 13 SCC 322

Case Note:

Arbitration - Proceedings - Interpretation of provision - Unregistered firm - Imposing of ban - Section 69(3) of Indian Partnership Act, 1932 - Respondent invited tenders for construction - Appellant/unregistered partnership firm was successful bidder - Dispute arose as between Appellant and Respondent - Appellant moved to High Court to restrain Respondent from dispossessing Appellant from work-site till work executed by Appellant was measured by Commissioner to be appointed by Court - Commissioner was appointed - Appellant filed another application to restrain Respondent from operating its bank accounts and from dispossessing Appellant - Arbitrator was appointed by Respondent to adjudicate dispute between them - Arbitration application was subsequently withdrawn - Claim of Appellant was allowed to certain extent along with interest - While resisting claim of Appellant, Respondent did not specifically raise any plea under Section 69 of Act, 1932 - Respondent challenged award before High Court by filing application which was dismissed by Single Judge by order - Respondent filed Review Application which was also dismissed by Single Judge - Pending disposal of appeals filed by Respondent, interim order was passed directing Respondent to deposit certain percent of decretal - By impugned order, Division Bench allowed appeals - Hence, present appeal - Whether expression other proceedings contained in Section 69(3) of Act, 1932 will include Arbitral proceedings and can be equated to suit filed in Court and thereby ban imposed against unregistered firm can operate in matter of arbitral proceedings

Facts:

The Respondent/Cooperative Group Housing Society invited tenders for construction of 102 dwelling units with basement. The Appellant/ unregistered partnership firm submitted its bid in response to the said tender. The Appellant was the successful bidder and the contract was awarded to the Appellant. The Appellant was issued a letter of intent. The Appellant submitted its first bill for the construction of the compound wall etc. The agreement for the construction of 102 dwelling units with basement was entered into between the Appellant and the Respondent. There was some delay in getting the plan sanctioned, which according to the Appellant, he was not responsible for the delay. A dispute arose as between the Appellant and the Respondent which necessitated the Appellant to move the High Court by way of an application under Section 9 of the Arbitration and Conciliation Act, 1996 to restrain the Respondent from dispossessing the Appellant from the worksite till the work executed by the Appellant is measured by the Commissioner to be appointed by the Court. A Commissioner was also appointed by the High Court. The Appellant filed another application under Section 9 of the Act to restrain the Respondent from operating its bank accounts and from dispossessing the Appellant. An arbitrator/an advocate was appointed by the Respondent to adjudicate the dispute between them. As the appointment came to be made by the Respondent, though, the Appellant earlier moved the High Court by way of an arbitration application under Section 11(5) of the Act for appointment of an independent arbitrator, the same was subsequently withdrawn. The Appellant participated in the arbitration proceedings before the arbitrator appointed by the Respondent. The claim of the Appellant was allowed to the certain extent along with interest. While resisting the claim of the Appellant, the Respondent did not specifically raise any plea under Section 69 of the Partnership Act, 1932. The Respondent challenged the award before the High Court by filing an application which was dismissed by the Single Judge by an order. The Respondent filed Review Application which was also dismissed by the Single Judge. As against these orders, the Respondent preferred appeals. Pending disposal of the appeals, an interim order was passed directing the Respondent to deposit 50 percent of the decretal. By the impugned order, the Division Bench having allowed the appeals, the Appellant filed present appeal.

Held, while allowing the appeal:

(i) The condition precedent for the operation of ban under Sub-section (3) is that the launching of a suit in a Court of law should be present and it should be by an unregistered firm or by a person claiming to be partner of an unregistered firm either to a claim for set off in the said suit or any other proceedings intrinsically connected with the said suit. The specific exclusions contained in Clauses (a) and (b) of Sub-section (3) therefore makes the position clear to the effect that even though such proceedings may fall under the expression "other proceedings" and may be intrinsically connected with a suit in a Court, yet the ban would not operate against such proceedings. [13] and[15]

(ii) The contract between the parties contained an Arbitration Clause. The Respondent invoked the said Clause and an Arbitrator came to be appointed. After the Respondent filed its statement of claim, the Appellant filed its reply and also its counter claim. Before the Arbitrator, in the course of oral arguments, a faint attempt was made contending that, the Appellant-firm being an unregistered one, by virtue of Section 69 of the Act, 1932 the proceedings insofar as the counter claim was concerned, the same was not maintainable and should be rejected. The Arbitrator took the correct view that Section 69 has no application to the proceedings of the Arbitrator and held that the objection of the Respondent was not sustainable. The Arbitrator allowed the counter claim to the certain extent. When the award of the Arbitrator was challenged by the Respondent under Section 34 of the Act, 1996 the very same objection was raised as a ground of attack. The Single Judge of the High Court also found no merit in the said contention and upheld the award of counter claim. [18]

(iii) The Division Bench took a contrary view and held that the counter claim in an Arbitral Proceedings is covered by the expression "other proceedings" contained in Section 69(3) of the Act, 1932 and the Appellant being an unregistered firm at the relevant point of time was hit by the embargo contained therein and consequently the award of counter claim in the award as confirmed by the learned Judge was reversed as not justiciable by virtue of Section 69 of the Act, 1932. [19]

(iv) In in order to attract the said Section, first and foremost the pending proceeding must be a suit instituted in a Court and in that suit a claim of set off or other proceedings will also be barred by virtue of the provision set out in Sub-sections (1) and (2) of Section 69 as specifically stipulated in Sub-section (3) of the said Section. Having regard to the manner in which the expressions are couched in Sub-section (3), a claim of set off or other proceedings cannot have independent existence. In other words, the foundation for the application of the said Sub-section should be the initiation of a suit in which a claim of set off or other proceedings which intrinsically connected with the suit arise and not otherwise. [20]

(v) It was held as to how a reading of Section 69 as a whole does not permit of any interpretation that would cover Arbitral proceedings, de hors, filing of a suit in a Court and that too in respect of a right under a contract governed by the provisions of the Act, 1932 especially after the coming into force of the Act, 1996 and the proceedings governed by the special features contained in the said Act. Therefore, any interpretation made under the Limitation Act while construing Section 14 to treat Arbitral proceedings on par with civil proceedings could not be applied to the case on hand. [32]

(vi) In the absence of such a specific provision, it will not be appropriate to import the definition Clause under Section 2(a) of the Interest Act to the Partnership Act in order to apply Section 69(3) of the Act, 1932. Going by Sections 35 and 36 of the Act, 1996 it could not be held that the entire Arbitral proceeding was a Civil Court proceedings for the purpose of applicability of Section 69(3) of the Act, 1932. [33] and[34]

(vii) Having regard to conclusion that Arbitral Proceedings will not come under the expression "other proceedings" of Section 69(3) of the Act, 1932, the ban imposed under the said Section 69 can have no application to Arbitral proceedings as well as the Arbitration Award. The impugned judgment of the Division Bench was set aside and the judgment of the Single Judge stands restored. [36]

CHAPTER SIX

V. Subramaniam vs. Rajesh Raghuvandra Rao (20.03.2009 - SC) : MANU/SC/0417/2009

Relative Section:

Indian Partnership Act, 1932 - Section 69; Code of Civil Procedure, 1908 (CPC) - Section 113

Hon'bleJudges/Coram:

Markandey Katju and G.S. Singhvi, JJ.

Equivalent Citation:AIR2009SC1858, 2009(3)BomCR790, 2009BusLR397(SC), 2009(3)CTC82, JT2009 (4)SC212,(2009)4MLJ120(SC),2009(2)RCR(Civil)622,2009(4)SCALE459, (2009)5SCC608, [2009] 5SCR 942 2009(4)UJ1712

NumberofPagesintheOriginalJudgment: 7

Case Reference:

Maneka Gandhi v. Union of India and Anr. MANU/SC/0133/1978; Chiranjit Lal Chowdhuri v. Union of India MANU/SC/0009/1950; Ananda Behera v. State of Orissa MANU/SC/0018/1955; Virendra Singh v. State of U.P. MANU/SC/0025/1954; Wazir Chand v. State of H.P. MANU/SC/0007/1954; Nathubhai Dhulaji v. Municipal Corporation MANU/MH/0103/1959; Vajrapuri Naidu, N. v. New Theatres, Carnatic Talkies Ltd. MANU/TN/0485/1959; Chintamanrao and Anr. v. The State of Madhya Pradesh MANU/SC/0008/1950; M.C.V.S. Arunachala Nadar v. State of Madras and Ors. MANU/SC/0030/1958; State of Madras v. V.G. Row MANU/SC/0013/1952; Jagdish Chandra Gupta v. Kajaria Traders (India)

Ltd. MANU/SC/0047/1964; Andhra Pradesh and Ors. v. P. Laxmi Devi MANU/SC/1017/2008

Case Note:

Constitution - Unregistered partnership - Dissolution of - Deprivation of property - Constitutional validity of Section 69(2A) - Sections 69, 69(1), 69(2), 69(2A) and 69(3) of Indian Partnership Act, 1932 - Section 113 of Code of Civil Procedure Code, 1908 - Articles 14, 19(1) and 300A of Constitution of India - Suit for dissolution of unregistered partnership between Appellant and Respondent filed by Appellant - Respondent contended suit not maintainable in view of Section 69(2A) of Indian Partnership Act - Trial Court held Section 69(2A) of the Act was unconstitutional being violative of Article 14 and 19(1)(g) of the Constitution - Reference made to High Court - High Court held Section 69(2A) not unconstitutional - Hence, present appeal - Held, in view of Sub-section 2A of Section 69 a partner in an unregistered partnership firm in State of Maharashtra cannot file suit for dissolution or for accounts of dissolved firm or realize properties of dissolved firm unless duration of firm was only six months or its capital upto Rs. 2000 only - Partnership firm, whether registered or unregistered, is not a distinct legal entity - Hence, property of firm really belongs to partners of firm - Sub-section 2A deprives partner of unregistered firm from recovery of his share in property of firm or from seeking dissolution of firm - Effect of Amendment is that partnership firm can come into existence and function without registration but cannot go out of existence - It will result in a situation where in case of disputes amongst partners the relationship of partnership cannot be put an end to by approaching Court of law - Dishonest partners, if in control of business or if stronger, can deprive other partners of his dues from partnership - Could result in extreme hardship and injustice - Aggrieved partner would be left without any remedy - Can neither file suit to compel mischievous partner to co-operate for registration nor resort to arbitration - Restrictions placed by Sub-section 2A of Section 69 introduced by Maharashtra Amendment Act arbitrary, excessive and cannot be regarded reasonable - Arbitrariness and unreasonableness violates Articles 14 and 19(1)(g) of the Constitution - Sub-section 2A of Section 69 as introduced by the Maharashtra Legislature clearly violates Articles 14, 19(1)(g) and 300A of the Constitution - It is ultra vires and unconstitutional - Impugned Judgment of High Court set aside - Suit to proceed - Appeal allowed

Ratio Decidendi:

"Sub-section 2A of Section 69 introduced by Maharashtra Partnership Amendment Act, 1984 which deprives a partner in an unregistered firm from recovery of his share in the property of the firm or from seeking dissolution of the firm is arbitrary and unreasonable and is violative of Articles 14 and 19(1)(g) of the Constitution."

Facts:

1. This appeal arises out of a suit filed before the Bombay City Civil Court instituted by the appellant praying inter alia for dissolution of an unregistered partnership firm between the appellant and the respondent. In that suit a defence taken was that the suit was not maintainable in view of Sub-section (2A) of Section 69 of the Indian Partnership Act, 1932 (hereinafter referred to as `the Act'). The Bombay City Civil Court was of the view that the said Sub-section 2A, which was introduced by the Maharashtra Amendment to Section 69 of the Act, being the Maharashtra Act No. 29 of 1984 (which received assent of the President of India) was unconstitutional being violative of Articles 14 and 19(1)(g) of the Constitution of India. Hence the Bombay City Civil Court by order dated 16.8.1999 made a reference to the High Court under Section 113 of C.P.C.[3]

Held, while allowing the appeal:

1. In our opinion the restrictions placed by Sub-section 2A of Section 69 introduced by the Maharashtra Amendment Act, for the reasons given above, are arbitrary and of excessive nature and go beyond what is in the public interest. Hence the restrictions cannot be regarded as reasonable.[27]

2. In the Constitution bench decision of this Court in Maneka Gandhi v. Union of India and Anr. (supra) it has been held that arbitrariness and unreasonableness violates Articles 14 and 19(1)(g) of the Constitution. The said provision is clearly unreasonable and arbitrary since by prohibiting suits for dissolution of an unregistered firm, for accounts and for realization of the properties of the firm, it creates a situation where businessmen will be very reluctant to enter into an unregistered partnership out of fear that they will not be able to recover the money they have invested in the firm or to get out of the firm if they wish to do so. As already stated above there is no legal requirement, unlike in England, which makes registration of a firm compulsory, rather in India it is voluntary. Both registered and unregistered are legal though of course registration and non registration have different legal consequences as stated above.[28]

3. The High Court was of the view that the object of the Maharashtra Amendment was to induce partners to register and it was intended to protect third party members of the public. We cannot see how Sub-section 2A of Section 69 in any way protects the third party members of the public. It makes it virtually impossible for partners in an unregistered firm to dissolve the firm or recover their share in the property of the firm. Hence it is totally arbitrary.[29]

4. It is true that it has been held by this Court in Government of Andhra Pradesh and Ors. v. P. Laxmi Devi MANU/SC/1017/2008 : AIR2008SC1640 that the Court should not lightly declare a statute to be unconstitutional as it expresses the will of the people through its elected representatives. However, that does not mean that a statute can never be declared as unconstitutional. In fact the aforesaid decision this Court has held that in some circumstances a statute can be declared as unconstitutional, namely, where it clearly violates some constitutional provision. Since in our opinion Sub-section 2A of Section 69 as introduced by the Maharashtra Legislature clearly violates Articles 14, 19(1)(g) and 300A of the Constitution, it is in our opinion ultra vires and is hence declared unconstitutional. Consequently this appeal is allowed and impugned judgment of the Bombay High Court is set aside. The suit can now proceed ignoring Sub-section 2A which we have declared invalid. No costs.[30]

CHAPTER SEVEN

Premlata and Ors. vs.Ishar Dass Chaman Lal and Ors. (10.01.1995 – SC) : MANU/ SC/0139/1995

Relative Section:

Arbitration Act, 1940 [repealed] - Section 20, Arbitration Act, 1940 [repealed] - Section 8; Indian Partnership Act, 1932 - Section 3(a), Indian Partnership Act, 1932 - Section 69, Indian Partnership Act, 1932 - Section 69(1), Indian Partnership Act, 1932 - Section 69(3)(a)

Hon'bleJudges/Coram:

K. Ramaswamy and S.V. Manohar, JJ.

Equivalent Citation: AIR1995SC714, 1995(3)ALT33(SC), 1995(1)ARBLR321(SC), I(1995)BC636(SC), I(1995)BC636(SC), JT1995(1)SC557, 19952RRR314, 1995(1)SCALE145, (1995)2SCC145, [1995]1SCR168, 1995(1)UJ421

NumberofPagesintheOriginalJudgment:4

Case Reference:

Jagdish Chander Gupta v. Kajaria Traders (India) Ltd., MANU/SC/ 0047/1964

Case Note:

Arbitration - jurisdiction - Partnership Act, 1932 and Section 20 of Arbitration Act, 1940 - enforcement of right to sue for dissolution includes right for reference to arbitration in terms of agreement of partnership by and between parties - party can enforce right by suit for rendering accounts and for realisation of property of dissolved firm - no prohibition to invoke arbitration clause under deed of partnership agreed to by and between parties to invoke Section 20 - held, suit under Section 20 maintainable.

Facts:

1. This appeal, by special leave, arises from the judgment of the learned Single Judge of the Punjab and Haryana High Court in Civil Revision No. 660/85, dated May 7, 1985.[2]

2. M/s. Ishar Das Chaman Lal - partnership firm consists of Ishar Das, the father, Chaman Lal and Om Prakash, his sons. By a deed of partnership dated 13.12.1965, the aforesaid partnership firm was constituted but the firm was not registered under Section 69 of the Indian Partnership Act. Chaman Lal, the eldest son died on 6.3.1978, by obvious reasons of which the partnership stood dissolved. By the death of one of the members, it is no longer possible to adhere to the original contract. The appellants - the widow and alleged son of the deceased Chaman Lal - called upon the respondents to render the accounts of the firm. Since they did not do so, invoking Clause (16) of the partnership deed, the appellants had called upon the respondents to refer the dispute to M/s. Tara Chand and Hans Raj Jain, Income-tax practitioners, the named arbitrators in the contract, to resolve the dispute: Since the respondents had refused to refer the dispute, the appellants invoked the jurisdiction of the civil court under Section 20 of the Arbitration Act, 1940, for short the Act. The respondents resisted the claim contending that since the partnership firm was an unregistered one, by operation of Section 69 of the Partnership Act, the application under Section 20 of the Act would not lie. The trial court negatived the contention of the respondents. But, on appeal and in revision, ultimately, the High Court held that Sub-section (1) of Section 69 and main part of Sub-section (3) of Section 69 exclude the application of Section 20 of the Act and consequently, the suit is not maintainable. Thus, this appeal, by special leave.[3]

Held, while allowing the appeal:

Thus this Court also had given effect to the exceptions carved out by Sub-sections (3) and (4) of Section 69 of the Partnership Act from the prohibition imposed by Sub-sections (1) and (2) and main part of Sub-section (3) even though the firm was not registered under Section 69.

1. It is seen that with the demise of the partners, ipso facto, the partnership stood dissolved. What the legal representatives of the deceased partner, is seeking to enforce is for accounts of a dissolved firm or any right or power to realise the property of the dissolved firm. The right 'to sue' for

the dissolution of the firm must, of necessity, be interpreted to mean the right to enforce the arbitration clause for resolution of the disputes relating to dissolved firm or for rendition of accounts or any right or power to realise the property of the dissolved firm.[8]

2. Indisputably the first appellant is the widow of Chaman Lal - one of the partners. Therefore, she steps into the shoes of the deceased partner who had a right in the dissolved partnership firm. Sub-section (3)(a) carves out three exceptions to Subsections (1) and (2) of Section 69 and also to the main part of Sub-section (3) of Section 69, namely, (1) the enforcement of any right to sue for the dissolution of firm; (2) for accounts of the dissolved firm; and (3) any right or power to realise the property of the dissolved firm. Having excluded from the embargo created by the main part of Sub-section (3) of Sub-sections (1) and (2) of Section 69, the right to sue would not again to be construed to engulf the exceptions carved out by Sub-section (3) or Sub-section (4) of Section 69 of the Act. Any construction otherwise would render the exceptions, legislature advisedly has carved out in Sub-sections (3) and (4) of Section 69, otiose. The object appears to be that the partnership having been dissolved or has come to a terminus, the rights of the parties are to be worked out in terms of the contract of the partnership entered by and between the partners and the rights engrafted therein. The exceptions carved out by Sub-section (3) are to enforce those rights including the rights to dissolution of the partnership despite the fact that the partnership firm was an unregistered one. Having kept that object in view, we are of the considered opinion that the alternative resolution forum agreed by the parties, namely, reference to a private arbitration is a mode of enforcing the rights given under Clause (a) of Sub-section (3) of Section 69 of the Act and gets excluded from the main part of Sub-section (3) and Sub-sections (1) and (2) of Section 69. The enforcement of the right to sue for dissolution includes a right for reference to an arbitration in terms of the agreement of the partnership by and between the parties. Therefore, there is no embargo for filing a suit under Section 20 of the Act.[9]

3. It is fairly stated by Shri Satish Chandra that the party can enforce the right by a suit for rendering accounts and for realisation of the property of the dissolved firm pro-rata. When that is permissible by an exception carved out by Sub-section (3)(a) to Section 69, we are of the view that there is no prohibition to invoke arbitration clause under the deed of partnership, agreed to by and between the parties to invoke Section 20 of the Act. Thus

considered, we are of the view that the suit under Section 20 of the Act is maintainable. The High Court has, therefore, committed manifest error of law in holding otherwise.[10]

The appeal is allowed with costs of Rs. 5,000.

4. Since we have allowed the appeal, we direct the trial court to send the reference immediately to the named arbitrators and we do hope that the arbitrators would immediately enter upon the reference and decide the dispute as expeditiously as possible within a period of 6 months from the date of the receipt of this order as this is a matter pending for long time.[11]

CHAPTER EIGHT

Arvind Constructions Co. Pvt. Ltd. vs. Kalinga Mining Corporation and Ors. (17.05.2007 - SC) : MANU/ SC/7697/2007

Relative Section:

Arbitration And Conciliation Act, 1996 - Section 11(4)(b), Arbitration And Conciliation Act, 1996 - Section 9; Indian Partnership Act, 1932 - Section 69(3); Specific Relief Act 1963 - Section 10, Specific Relief Act 1963 - Section 14, Specific Relief Act 1963 - Section 41, Specific Relief Act 1963 - Section 42

Hon'bleJudges/Coram:

Tarun Chatterjee and P.K. Balasubramanyan, JJ.

Equivalent   Citation:

AIR2007SC2144,2008(3)ALT1(SC),2007(2)ARBLR279(SC),2007 (3) CCC 239, JT 2007 (8)SC32, 2008(1)MhLj7, 2008(1)MhLJ7(SC), 2007(3)RCR(Civil)773, 2007(7)SCALE567, (2007) 6SCC 798, [2007]7SCR180

NumberofPagesintheOriginalJudgment: 6

Case Reference:

Arbitration And Conciliation Act, 1996 - Section 11(4)(b), Arbitration And Conciliation Act, 1996 - Section 9; Indian Partnership Act, 1932 - Section 69(3); Specific Relief Act 1963 - Section 10, Specific Relief Act 1963

- Section 14, Specific Relief Act 1963 - Section 41, Specific Relief Act 1963 - Section 42

Case Note:

(1)Arbitration and Conciliation Act, 1996 - Section 9--Interim measure--District Court while entertaining application under Section 9 directing parties to maintain status quo--After hearing parties, order of maintaining status quo directed to continue until arbitral Tribunal constituted to take up disputes between parties--On appeal, High Court took view that District Court in error in granting order to maintain status quo since prima facie agreement between parties not specifically enforceable in terms of Specific Relief Act--And since term of agreement had expired, it was not proper to grant interim order--Thus, High Court reserved order of District Court and dismissed application of appellant company under Section 9--Whether any interference called for at this interlocutory stage?--Held, "no".

(2)Arbitration and Conciliation Act, 1996 - Section 9--Interim measure/relief -- District Court entertaining application under Section 9--Shall have same power for making orders as it has for purpose and in relation to any proceedings before it--General rules governing grant of interim injunction at threshold--Attracted even while dealing with application under Section 9--Act does not prima facie purport to keep out provisions of Specific Relief Act--Exercise of power under Section 9--Must be based on well recognised principles governing grant of interim injunctions and other orders of interim protection or appointment of receiver.

Ratio Decidendi: Interim orders-Powers of Court-Applicability of principles

Facts:

1. M/s Kalinga Mining Corporation, a partnership firm bearing registration No. 71/1949, came into existence on 10.12.1949. During the years from 1973 to 1980, the firm obtained three mining leases from the State Government. The partnership firm was reconstituted in the year 1980, taking in some additional partners, again in the year 1991 and yet again in the year 1994. [2]

2. On 14.3.1991, the firm entered into an agency agreement with the appellant, a private limited company for a term of 10 years. Thereby, the appellant was engaged as a raising contractor in respect of the mines for which the firm had obtained leases from the State Government. On 25.3.1991, the firm executed an irrevocable Power of Attorney in favour of the appellant authorizing it to administer the mines and sell the iron ore

extracted there from.[3]

3. On 13.3.2001, the term of 10 years fixed in the agency agreement expired. New terms were negotiated between the parties and on 22.9.2001, the agreement was extended for a period of three years commencing from 14.3.2001. The term was to end with 31.3.2003. Again, on 3.9.2003, the term of the agreement was extended for a further period of three years commencing from 1.4.2003. Thereby, the period was to end with 31.3.2006.[4]

4. The appellant sought a further extension of the term of the agency agreement. Apparently, the firm was not willing for an extension. Certain disputes thus arose and by letter dated 19.11.2005, the appellant-company sought resolution of the said disputes. The appellant- company followed this up by a letter dated 9.12.2005 invoking the arbitration clause in the agency agreement and nominating Mr. Sanjeev Jain as its arbitrator in terms of the arbitration agreement.[5]

Held, while allowing the appeal:

1. It is seen that in spite of the parties naming their respective arbitrators, in terms of the arbitration agreement, more than one year back, the arbitrators so appointed had not been able to nominate a Presiding Arbitrator in terms of the arbitration agreement. We therefore put it to counsel on both sides as to why we shall not constitute an Arbitral Tribunal in view of their failure to constitute the Arbitral Tribunal in terms of the arbitration agreement and in view of the urgency involved in resolving the disputes between the parties. Counsel on both sides agreed that this Court may appoint either a Presiding Arbitrator or a sole arbitrator for the purpose of resolving the disputes between the parties. A panel of names was furnished. Having considered the names shown therein and taking note of the submissions at the bar, we think that it would be appropriate and just to both the parties to appoint Mr. Justice Y.K. Sabharwal, former Chief Justice of India as the sole arbitrator for deciding all the disputes between the parties. We therefore appoint Mr. Justice Y.K. Sabharwal, former Chief Justice of India as the sole arbitrator to decide on the disputes between the parties springing out the agreement dated 14.3.1991 and the Power of Attorney dated 25.3.1991. The arbitrator would be free to fix his terms in consultation with the parties. We would request the arbitrator to expeditiously decide the dispute on entering upon the reference and to give his award as early as possible. [16]

2. In the result, we decline to interfere with the order of the High Court and dismiss this appeal. While doing so, we revoke the nomination made by the parties of two arbitrators. We appoint Mr. Justice Y.K. Sabharwal, former Chief Justice of India as the sole arbitrator to decide the dispute between the parties. The parties are directed to suffer their respective costs.[17]

CHAPTER NINE

Kamal Pushp Enterprises vs. D.R. Construction Company (28.07.2000 - SC) : MANU/SC/0465/2000

Relative Section:

Arbitration Act, 1940 [repealed] - Section 14(2), Arbitration Act, 1940 [repealed] - Section 2(a), Arbitration Act, 1940 [repealed] - Section 8(2); Indian Partnership Act, 1932 - Section 69, Indian Partnership Act, 1932 - Section 69(2), Indian Partnership Act, 1932 - Section 69(3)

Hon'bleJudges/Coram:

M. Jagannadha Rao and Doraiswamy Raju, JJ.

Equivalent Citation: AIR2000SC2676, 2000(5)ALT39(SC), 2000(3)ARBLR1(SC), 2001(2)JLJ130(SC), JT2000(8)SC347,2001-1-LW569,2000(4)RCR(Civil)75,2000(5) SCALE348,(2000)6SCC659,[2000]Supp 2SCR 20 , 2000(2)UJ1250

NumberofPagesintheOriginalJudgment: 4

Case Reference:

Arbitration - bar of suit - Section 69 (2) of Partnership Act, 1932 - whether Section 69 bar right of unregistered firm from defending proceedings against it - Section 69 precludes only initiation of proceedings by such firm - bar does not stand in way of unregistered firm defending proceedings against it.

Case Note:

Arbitration - bar of suit - Section 69 (2) of Partnership Act, 1932 - whether Section 69 bar right of unregistered firm from defending proceedings against it - Section 69 precludes only initiation of proceedings by such firm - bar does not stand in way of unregistered firm defending proceedings against it.

Facts:

1. The Gas Authority of India Ltd., at Vijaypur, entered into a contract with the appellant to execute certain works and the appellant in its turn had entered into a separate contract with the respondent, indisputably an unregistered firm for carrying out the work, the execution of which was undertaken by the appellant under its contract with 'GAIL'. Disputes arose between the appellant and the respondent. Thereupon, the appellant appears to have, invoking Section 8(2) of the Arbitration Act, 1940, served a notice on the respondent seeking for consent for the appointment of an Arbitrator, in terms of the arbitration clause, out of five proposed Arbitrators and the respondent gave its consent for the appointment of a named Advocate, as the Arbitrator. The Arbitrator entered into the reference and the appellant filed its claim and the respondent apart from opposing the claim of the appellant stated its own claim. The Arbitrator passed an Award in favour of the respondent and suo moto filed the Award before the trial court under Section 14(2) of the Arbitration Act. When the Court issued notice to both the appellant and the respondent, it is at this stage the appellant filed various objections, one of which was based upon Section 69 of the Partnership Act, and the trial court appears to have framed a preliminary issue of law under Order 14 Rule 2, CPC, for decision as follows:[2]

Whether the proceedings regarding making the award rule of Court are maintainable as the non-applicant firm is not a registered partnership firm under Section 69 of the Partnership Act?

Held, while allowing the appeal:

1. The prohibition contained in Section 69 is in respect of instituting a proceeding to enforce a right arising from a contract in any Court by an unregistered firm, and it had no application to the proceedings before an Arbitrator and that too when the reference to the Arbitrator was at the instance of the appellant itself. If the said bar engrafted in Section 69 is absolute in its terms and is destructive of any and every right arising under the contract itself and not confined merely to enforcement of a right arising from a contract by an unregistered firm by instituting a suit or other proceedings in Court only, it would become a jurisdictional issue in respect of the Arbitrator's power, authority and competency itself, undermining

thereby the legal efficacy of the very award, and consequently furnish a ground by itself to challenge the award when it is sought to be made a rule of Court. The case before us cannot be said to be one such and the learned Counsel for the appellant though was fully conscious of this fact, yet tried to assert that it is open to the appellant to take up the objection based upon Section 69 of the Partnership Act, at any stage - even during the post award proceedings to enforce the award passed. The Award in this case cannot either rightly or legitimately said to be vitiated on account of the prohibition contained in Section 69 of the Partnership Act, 1932 since the same has no application to proceedings before an Arbitrator. At the stage of enforcement of the award by passing a decree in terms thereof what is enforced is the award itself which crystallise the rights of parties under the Indian Contract Act and the general law to be paid for the work executed and not any right arising only from the objectionable contract. It is useful in this connection to refer to the decision of this Court in Satish Kumar and Ors. v. Surinder Kumar and Ors. MANU/SC/0264/1968 : [1969]2SCR244 , wherein it has been stated in unmistakable terms that an Award is not a mere waste paper but does create rights and has some legal effect besides being final and binding on the parties. It has also been held that the Award is, in fact, a final adjudication of a Court of the parties' own choice and until impeached upon sufficient grounds in an appropriate proceedings, an Award which is on the face of it regular, is conclusive upon the merits of the controversy submitted for Arbitration. Consequently, the post Award proceedings cannot be considered by any means, to be a suit or other proceedings to enforce any rights arising under a contract. All the more so when, as in this case, at all stages the respondent was only on the defence and has not itself instituted any proceedings to enforce any rights of the nature prohibited under Section 69 of the Partnership Act, before any Court as such. We see no infirmity or error whatsoever in the decision of the courts below to call for our interference in this appeal. The appeal fails and shall stand dismissed.[9]

2. We make it clear that we have decided only the point relating to the preliminary issue raised and decided by the trial judge as well as by the High Court, and all or any other objections and contentions may be raised and pursued by the respective parties in the proceedings pending before the trial court. The parties will bear their respective costs.[10]

CHAPTER TEN

Firm Ashok Traders and Ors. vs. Gurumukh Das Saluja and Ors. (09.01.2004 - SC) : MANU/SC/0026/2004

Relative Section:

Arbitration Act, 1940 [repealed] - Section 20; Arbitration And Conciliation Act, 1996 - Section 11, Arbitration And Conciliation Act, 1996 - Section 17, Arbitration And Conciliation Act, 1996 - Section 2, Arbitration And Conciliation Act, 1996 - Section 36, Arbitration And Conciliation Act, 1996 - Section 37(1)(a), Arbitration And Conciliation Act, 1996 - Section 9, Arbitration And Conciliation Act, 1996 - Section 9(ii)(d); Indian Partnership Act, 1932 - Section 69, Indian Partnership Act, 1932 - Section 69(3)

Hon'bleJudges/Coram:
R.C. Lahoti and Ashok Bhan, JJ.

Equivalent   **Citation:**
2004(16)AIC129,AIR2004SC1433,2004(1)ARBLR141(SC),2004(2) AWC 949 (SC) , (2004) 2CompLJ419(SC), (2004)2CompLJ419(SC), 2004(2)CTC208, 2004(I)CLR(SC)433, 2005 (2) JL J269 (SC), JT2004(2)SC352, 2004(3)MhLj592, 2004(3)MhLJ592(SC), 2004(1)MPJR(SC)268, 2004MPLJ266(SC), (2004)137PLR526,2004(1)RCR(Civil)725,2004(1)SCALE297, (2004)3SCC155, [2004]50SCL224(SC), [2004] 1SCR404

NumberofPagesintheOriginalJudgment: 12

Case Reference: V.T. Sipahimalani v. Kanta, MANU/SC/0067/2000; Sundaram Finance Ltd. v. NEPC India Ltd., MANU/SC/0012/1999; Kamal Pushpa Enterprises v. Dr Construction Company MANU/SC /0465/2000; Jagdish Chandra v. Kajaria Traders (Ind.) Ltd. MANU/SC/0047/1964; Shreeram Finance Corporation Ltd. v. Yasin Khan and Ors., MANU/SC/ 0341/1989; Delhi Development Authority v. Kochhar Construction Work and Anr., MANU/SC/1279/1998

Case Note:

(1) Indian Partnership act, 1932 - Section 69 (3)--Arbitration and Conciliation Act, 1996--Section 9--Unregistered firm--Application under Section 9 of Arbitration Act for interim measure of protection--Whether maintainable in view of bar of Section 69 (3) of Partnership Act?--Held, "yes" prima facie--Application under Section 9 is not suit--Right conferred under Section 9 is on party to arbitration agreement--Section 69 of Partnership Act has no bearing on right of party to arbitration clause to file application under Section 9 of Arbitration Act.

Prima facie, the bar enacted by Section 69 of the Partnership Act, 1932 in case of registered firm does not affect maintainability of an application under Section 9 of the Arbitration and Conciliation Act, 1996 (A and C Act). (A and C Act), 1996 is a long leap in the direction of alternate dispute resolution systems. It is based on UNCITRAL Model. The decided cases under the preceding Act of 1940 have to be applied with caution for determining the issues arising for decision under the new Act. An application under Section 9 under the scheme of A and C Act, is not a suit. Undoubtedly, such application results in initiation of civil proceedings but can it be said that a party filing an application under Section 9 of the Act is enforcing a right arising from a contract? "Party" is defined in clause (h) of sub-section (1) of Section 2 of A and C Act to mean 'a party to an arbitration agreement'. So, the right conferred by Section 9 is on a party to an arbitration agreement. The time or the stage for invoking the jurisdiction of Court under Section 9 can be (i) before, or (ii) during arbitral proceedings, or (iii) at any time after the making of the arbitral award but before it is enforced in accordance with Section 36. The right conferred by Section 9 cannot be saidto be one arising out of a contract. The qualification which the person invoking jurisdiction of the Court under Section 9 must possess is of being a 'party' to an arbitration agreement. A person not party to an arbitration agreement cannot enter the Court for protection under Section 9. This has relevance only to his locus standi as an applicant. This has nothing to do with the relief which is sought for from the Court or the right which is sought to be canvassed in support of the relief. The relief's which the Court may allow to a party under clauses (i) and (ii) of Section 9 flow from the power vesting in the Court exercisable by reference to 'contemplated', 'pending' or 'completed' arbitral proceedings. The Court is conferred with the same power for making the specified orders as it has for the purpose of and in relation to any proceedings before it though the venue of the proceedings in relation to which the power under Section 9 is sought to be exercised is the arbitral tribunal. Under the scheme of A and C Act, the arbitration clause is separable from other clauses of the partnership deed. The arbitration clause constitutes an agreement by itself. In short, filing of an application by a party by virtue of its being a party to an arbitration agreement is for securing a relief which the Court has power to grant before, during or after arbitral proceedings by virtue of Section 9 of the A and C Act. The relief sought for in an application under Section 9 of A and C Act, is neither in a suit nor a right arising from a contract. The right arising from the partnership deed or conferred by the Partnership Act, is being enforced in the arbitral Tribunal ; the court under Section 9 is only formulating interim measures so as to protect the right under adjudication before the arbitral Tribunal from being frustrated. Section 69 of the Partnership Act, has no bearing on the right of a party to an arbitration clause to file an application under Section 9 of A and C Act.

(2) Arbitration and Conciliation Act, 1996--Section 9--Application for appointment of receiver under Section 9--Serious matter to appoint receiver for running business--Condition to make application before commencement of arbitral proceedings--Applicant has not taken any step--Direction to take steps for appointment of arbitrator(s)--Though order of High Court appointing receiver maintained -- Certain directions issued.

Section 9 of the Arbitration and Conciliation Act, 1996, permits application being filed in the court before the commencement of the arbitral proceedings but the provision does not give any indication of how much before. The word 'before' means, inter alia, 'ahead of'; in presence or sight of; under the consideration or cognizance of'. The two events sought to be interconnected by use of the term 'before' must have proximity of relationship by reference to occurrence ; the later event proximately following the preceding event as a foreseeable or 'within sight' certainty. The party invoking Section 9 may not have actually commenced the arbitral proceedings but must be able to satisfy the court that the arbitral proceedings are actually contemplated or manifestly intended and are positively going to commence within a reasonable time. What is a reasonable time will depend on the facts and circumstances of each case and the nature of interim relief sought for would itself give an indication thereof. The distance of time must not be such as would destroy the proximity of relationship of the two events between which it exists and elapses.

The party having succeeded in securing an interim measure of protection before arbitral proceedings cannot afford to sit and sleep over the relief, conveniently forgetting the 'proximately contemplated' or 'manifestly intended' arbitral proceedings itself. If arbitral proceedings are not commenced within a reasonable time of an order under Section 9, the relationship between the order under Section 9 and the arbitral proceedings would stand snapped and the relief allowed to the party shall cease to be an order made 'before', i.e., in contemplation of arbitral proceedings. The court, approached by a party with an application under Section 9, is justified in asking the party and being told how and when the party approaching the court proposes to commence the arbitral proceedings. Rather, the scheme in which Section 9 is placed, obligates the court to do so. The court may also, while passing an order under Section 9 ,put the party on terms and may recall the order if the party commits breach of the terms.

Facts:

1. The dispute is among 12 persons who are, or are alleged to be, or claim to be partners in the firm M/s Ashok Traders, the respondent No. 1. These/ 12 private parties to the litigation can be grouped into three, for the sake of convenience. Gurumukh Das Saluja, Sanjay Chawla and Ajay Arora shall be collectively referred to as Group "A". Bhagwati Prasad Kulhara, Badri Prasad Jaiswal and Harprasad Jaiswal shall be referred to as Group "B". Rajesh Jaiswal, Ram Sewak Sharma, Baljeet Singh Bhatia, Rajendra Prasad Jaiswal, Anil Kumar Shrivastava and Sushil Kumar Shrivastava shall be referred to as Group "C".[2]

2. M/s. Ashok Traders are in liquor trade. In the Deed of Partnership entered into on 27.2.2002 there were 7 partners including Bhagwati Prasad Kulhara and 6 others. The partnership firm was registered with Registrar of Firms. Six partners (i.e. other than Bhagwati Prasad Kulhara) retired from the partnership and a new partnership came to be constituted on 5.3.2002 evidenced by a Deed of the even date wherein all the persons belonging to Groups A, B and C are partners. However, the names of the

new partners were not communicated to the Registrar of Firms. This firm was awarded a liquor contract licence for Bhopal for the year 2002-03 at a licence fee of Rs. 66.51 crores. The existence of these two Deeds of Partnership and the factum of the first one being registered and the second one being not registered with the Registrar of Firms are admitted facts. For convenience sake, we would refer to the partnership dated 27.2.2002 as Partnership - I, the Partnership dated 5,3.2002 as Partnership - II and the alleged partnership dated 6.3.2003 as Partnership - III.[3]

3. The business ran smoothly upto February 2003 and then differences and disputes are alleged to have arisen amongst the partners. Clause 20 of the Partnership Deed-II incorporates an Arbitration Clause. Group "B" alleges the existence of yet another Deed of Partnership which is dated 6.3.2003 wherein the names of the members of Group "A" are not to be found mentioned as partners. This partnership-ill is also not registered.[4]

4.On 6.3.2003 auction for IMFL and country-liquor shops (60 in number) for the year 2003-04 was held at Bhopal. M/s Ashok Traders was declared to be successful bidder for a licence fee of Rs. 73.25 crores. The shops are running and have always remained operational even during the present litigation.[5]

5. Disputes arose giving rise to complaints by the members of Group "A" complaining of the violation of their rights as partners at the hands of Group "B". Group "A" complained of their being denied access to accounts, of Group "B" indulging into mismanagement of affairs and siphoning off of the funds and so on. Ajay Arora (of Group "A") filed a civil suit which was held to be not-maintainable in view of Section 69(3) of the Indian Partnership Act, 1932; the name of Ajay Arora having not been shown in the Register of Firms as a partner of the firm. According to Group "A", a notice was issued on 2.6.2003 to the other partners invoking the arbitration clause and calling upon them to join in the appointment of arbitrator/s consistently with the arbitration clause so as to adjudicate upon the disputes between the partners. The contesting respondents do not admit the receipt of the notice. On 22.7.2003, Gurumukh Das Saluja of Group "A" filed an application under Section 9 of The Arbitration and Conciliation Act, 1996 wherein the principal relief sought for is the appointment of a receiver under Section 9(ii)(d) of the Act to take charge of the entire business of the firm. Other incidental injunctions are also sought for. Group "B" contested the application on very many grounds and mainly by submitting that the application was not maintainable in view of the bar enacted by Section

69(3) of the Partnership Act as the name of the applicant does not figure in the Register of Firms as partner of the firm. The plea has prevailed with the learned Additional District Judge resulting in dismissal of the application. Gurumukh Das Saluja preferred an appeal before the High Court under Section 37(1)(a) of the A & C Act. During the pendency of the appeal an application under Section 9 pleading similar facts and seeking similar reliefs, as was done before the Trial Court, was filed. Group "8" contested the application on all possible grounds. The factum of Group "A" being partners of the firm so far as the contract for the year 2003-04 is concerned was vehemently denied. It was reiterated that the application was hit by Section 69(3) of the Partnership Act and hence was liable to be dismissed. The High Court has allowed the appeal. It has held that the applicability of Section 69(3) is not attracted to an application under Section 9 of A & C Act. But on merits the High Court has found substance in the grievance raised by Group "A". The High Court has also held that the business in the year 2003-04 was continuing under the Partnership Deed dated 5.3.2002, i.e., Partnership - II; and that prima facie the existence of the Partnership Deed dated 6.3.2003 (Partnership - III) was doubtful and accompanied by suspicious circumstances raising doubts about the genuineness of any new partnership having come into existence on 6.3.2003 superseding the Partnership -II. The High Court seems to have made efforts at resolving the controversy and finding out at least some such solution as would take care of the disputes for the moment and protect the interests of all the parties and then concluded as under:-[6]

Held, while allowing the appeal:

1. During the course of hearing, we asked the learned counsel for the parties if either of them could suggest a practically feasible mechanism which would work and also effectively protect the interest of the parties kept away from the actual running of the business but no concrete suggestion came forward. On behalf of Group "A", a suggestion was mooted that $1/5^{th}$ of the shops may be allowed to be run by them and remaining $4/5^{th}$ may be allowed to be run by Group "B" and identical precautionary or protective mechanism may be introduced as cross-checks. But, what would be the mechanism, none has been able to propound and project [21].

2. As a result, the order under appeal is modified. Though the order of the High Court appointing 3 receiver on the partnership business is maintained, the rest of the order is set aside and substituted by the following directions: -[22]

(1) The business shall run as before under the actual management and control of Group "B" but as receivers.

(2) The Commissioner of Excise, Madhya Pradesh shall appoint an official who has been associated with the excise department of Madhya Pradesh, preferably a retired person, who shall act as an observer. The observer shall keep a watch on the business of M/s. Ashok Traders generally and in particular to see :

(i) that the business is run by receivers without any hindrance by any of the partners;

(ii) that the accounts are properly, truly and correctly maintained,

(iii) that the receipts and payments are properly vouched,

(iv) that the sale proceeds are properly accounted for and no part of the proceeds is siphoned off and/or carried away unaccounted by anyone.

(3) All the sale proceeds shall, be deposited day to day in a bank account to be opened in a nationalised bank in the name of the 'Firm M/s Ashok Traders (under orders of the Court)'. Any amounts to be withdrawn shall be only under the joint signatures of at least one members of Group "B" or "C" and the observer, for the purpose of making payments to the State Government, and on account of rent/licence fee of the shops, salary of the staff, transport charges and other necessary expenses required for running day to day business.

(4) Though the conduct of the business is being allowed to be continued by Group "B" but that is in their capacity of receivers as appointed by the Court. They must truly and strictly perform their duties as receivers. Any deviation would be viewed seriously.

(5) The members of Group "A" and/or their representative/s, authorized in writing, shall have a reasonable right to visit the shops during business hours and watch the activities going on but without interfering with the business activities run by the receivers.

(6) The observer shall be paid such monthly remuneration and reimbursed such expenses, as may be considered reasonable and appointed by the Commissioner at Excise subject to overall directions of the Trial Court.

(7) This arrangement shall continue till 31st March 2004 and also for such further period as may be necessary for winding up of the business as per terms of the license of the State Government (Excise Department).

(8) On finalization of the accounts duly audited by Chartered Accountants the net profit or loss, if any, shall be distributed in accordance

with the award given by the arbitrator or decision by any competent forum.

(9) The receivers and observers shall be under the control of the trial Court. In case of any difficulty in carrying out this order, the parties, the observer and the Excise Commissioner of Madhya Pradesh or any officer subordinate to him shall be at liberty to seek directions from the trial Court.

(10). Before parting we would like to clarify that whatever has been stated hereinabove in this order is not in any manner intended to be a reflection, much less a finding, on the merits of the case of either party which shall be available to be determined on evidence and material brought on record in any duly constituted legal proceedings whether before the arbitral tribunal or before the Court or any other forum. All that has been said hereinabove is by way of prima facie observations confined to the disposal of the present appeals.[23]

(11). The appeals stand disposed of. No order as to the costs.[24]

Syndicate Bank vs. R.S.R. Engineering Works and Ors. (09.05.2003 - SC) : MANU/ SC/0404/2003

Relative Section:

Indian Partnership Act, 1932 - Section 32, Indian Partnership Act, 1932 - Section 32(2), Indian Partnership Act, 1932 - Section 32(3), Indian Partnership Act, 1932 - Section 72

Hon'bleJudges/Coram:

Shivaraj V. Patil and K.G. Balakrishnan, JJ.

EquivalentCitation : 2003(7)AIC76,2003(4)ALD62(SC),2003(3) BLJR1677,[2003(3)JCR162(SC)],JT 2003 (4)SC578, 2003-4-LW684, 2003(3)PLJR160, (2003)134PLR570, 2003(3)RCR(Civil)81, 2003(4)SCALE648, (2003)6SCC265, [2003]Supp1SCR213

NumberofPagesintheOriginalJudgment:4

Case Reference:

Thummaia Rama Rao and Ors. v. Chodagam Venkateswara Rao and Ors., MANU/AP/0102/1963

Case Note:

Indian Partnership Act, 1932 Section 32 - The case debates the scope for a bank to proceed against its debtors, in this case a partnership firm, for recovery of debts.- An agreement was formed between the partners and the appellant bank for obtaining loan from the bank.- On nonpayment, the appellant bank filed a suit against all the partners including two of the partners who had retired from the firm.- The retired partners said that they were not liable since the entire liability of the firm rested with the fourth partner.- The Trial Court did not decree the suit against the second and third respondents who had retired from the firm.- The ruling of the Trial Court was sustained by the High Court.- However, the Supreme Court went against the rulings of the Trial Court and the High Court and permitted the Bank to proceed against all the defendants in the suit.

Facts:

1. The plaintiff appellant filed two suit against the respondents. First respondent in both the suits is a partnership firm engaged in engineering works. Respondent Nos. 2 to 4 are its partners. In the first suit, O.S. No. 1921/80 which was filed for recovery of Rs. 59,775.95 with interest thereon, the plaintiff alleged that for the purpose of expansion of industry of the respondent, a loan of Rs. 40,000/- was sanctioned in favour of the respondents on 5.12.1974. The loan was to be re-paid after 9 months in installments. They respondents had also executed the requisite documents in favour of the plaintiff bank. Respondent Nos. 2 and 3 in their written statement admitted that the respondents had borrowed Rs. 40,000/- from the appellant, but they contended that the first respondent firm was dissolved and the fourth respondent took over the entire liability and, therefore , they are not liable for the suit claim. The Trial Court passed the decree only against Respondent-1 and Respondent-4 for the suit claim.

2. The appellant filed a Regular First Appeal No. 632/87 before the High Court and prayed that decree shall be passed against all the respondents as all of them had joint and several liability. This plea was rejected by the High Court and the High Court affirmed the decree of the trial court. Aggrieved by the same, Civil Appeal No. 3765 f 1995 is filed.

3. In O.S. No. 1922/80 filed against these respondent, the plaintiff alleged that these respondents were given an overdraft facility to the extent of Rs. 20,000/- by the appellant bank and that the respondent availed that facility and omitted default in paying the amount due from them and, therefore, the appellant filed the suit for recovery of Rs. 35,157,68/- with interest thereon. The respondents raised similar contention that the partnership was dissolved and the fourth respondent had taken over the entire liability and that the respondent Nos. 2 and 3 stood absolved of the suit liability. The Trial court accepted this contention and passed a decree in favour of the plaintiff against respondent Nos. 1 and 4. Aggrieved and the same, the appellant filed a Regular First Appeal being RFA No. 631/87 before the High Court and the High Court affirmed the trial court decree by

its judgment and aggrieved by the same, Civil Appeal No. 1337 of 1995 is filed.

Held, while allowing the appeal:

1. In the instant case, at the time when the partners entered into the agreement for overdraft facility, they were to members of the partnership firm; so also defendants 2 to 4 jointly executed an agreement and obtain loan from the bank. Subsequent retirement of defendants 2 and 3 is of no consequence unless there is a subsequence contract between these members of the partnership firm and the plaintiff. The law on this aspect is succinctly made clear in the celebrated book "Lindley & Bank on Partnership (Sixteenth Edition) and at page 358, it is stated as under:[8]

"It is perhaps self evident that a creditor's rights will not normally be prejudiced by an agreement transferring an accrued liability from one partner to another unless the creditor is made a party to the agreement or assents to its operation. Otherwise the agreement will, as regards him, be strictly res inter alios acta. Lord Lindley illustrated this proposition for the following example:

--let it be supposed that a firm of three members, A, B, and c, is indebted to D; that a retires, and B and C either alone, or together with a new partner, E, take upon themselves the liabilities of the old firm. D's right to obtain payment form A, B, and C is not affected by the by arrangement, and A does not cease to be liable to him for the debt in question. But if, after A's retirement, D accepts as his sole debtors B and C, or B, C, and E (if E enters the firm), then A's liability will have ceased, and D must look for payment to B and C, or to B, C and E, as the case may be."

2. There is no a priori presumption to the effect that the creditors of firm do, on the retirement of a partner, enter into an agreement to discharge him from liability. An adoption by the creditor of the new firm as his debtor does not by any mean necessarily deprive him or his rights against the old firm especially when the creditor is not a party to the arrangement and then there is no fresh agreement between the creditor and the newly constituted firm. After the creditor has taken a new security for a debt from a continuing partner, it may be a strong a evidence of an intention to look only the continuing partner for the payment due form the firm.[9]

3. It is also important to note that it has long been recognised that partnership is not a species of joint tenancy and that, in the absence of some contrary agreement, there is no survivorship as between partners, at least so far as it concerns their beneficial interests in the partnership assets.[10]

4. Having due regard to these principles, the High Court erred in confirming the judgment passed by the trial court and the plaintiff appellant had every right to proceed against all the defendants in the suit. Hence, the appeals are allowed and the impugned decree is modified to the extent that there shall be a decree against all the respondents, namely respondent 1 to 4, both the suits.[11]

5. The appeals are allowed with costs.[12]

Krishna Motor Service vs. H.B. Vittala Kamath (19.04.1996 – SC) : MANU/ SC/0558/1996

Relative Section:

Arbitration Act, 1940 [repealed] - Section 20, Arbitration Act, 1940 [repealed] - Section 8, Arbitration Act, 1940 [repealed] - Section 8(1); Indian Partnership Act, 1932 - Section 69, Indian Partnership Act, 1932 - Section 69(1), Indian Partnership Act, 1932 - Section 69(3)

Hon'bleJudges/Coram:

K. Ramaswamy and G.B. Pattanaik, JJ.

Equivalent Citation: AIR1996SC2209, 1996(2)ARBLR1(SC), 1996 (2) CCC 418 , JT1996(5)SC162, 19962RRR586, 1996(4)SCALE412, (1996)10SCC88, [1996]Supp1SCR594

NumberofPagesintheOriginalJudgment:4

Case Reference:

Jagdish Chander Gupta v. Kajaria Traders (India) Ltd. MANU/SC/0047/ 1964; Mahendra Lal Kushiary v. Gurdeyal Singh, AIR 1951 Pat 196, ILR 30 Pat 109; Prem Lata v. Ishar Dass Chaman Lal MANU/SC/0139/1995

Case Note:

Arbitration - validity - Section 69 (3) of Partnership Act, 1932 and Section 20 of Arbitration Act, 1940 - matte pertaining to applicability of exceptions to sub-section (3) of Section 69 - partnership firm not registered under Section 69 - as per law prescribed, taking out true and correct account of profit and loss of concerned firm and carve out share of petitioner - if respondent willing to continue firm in the same name which it had without taking petitioner as partner - petitioner entitle to compensation only up to date of dissolution of firm and not there after - above provisions falls within exception of said Section in present case - appeal accordingly allowed.

Facts:

1. These appeals by special leave arise from the order of a Division Bench of the Karnataka High Court made in M.F.A. No. 324/86 on 3.1.1994 and in Civil Petition No. 96/94 on 25.3.1994. It is not necessary to narrate in extenso the constitution, existence and continuance of the partnership firm prior to July 1, 1973. Suffice it to state that the respondent, who was working in the partnership firm as a Supervisor on salary basis, was taken as a partner on July 1, 1973, resulting a new partnership and it was agreed that he would be entitled to 10% of the profit and loss without contribution of any capital in the partnership. When disputes had arisen between the appellants and the respondent, the appellants - four partners - had a notice issued on 10.5.1984 dissolving the partnership. The respondent by his reply dated 17.5.1984 had agreed for dissolution. Subsequently, he filed an application under Section 20 of the Arbitration Act, 1940 (for short, the 'Act) on 8.6.1984, in the court of the Civil Judge at Shimoga for reference to the arbitrator in terms of the agreement. The Trial Court rejected three out of 4 claims made by him and referred claim No. 1 to the arbitration. The High Court on further consideration, in appeal, added two more items to the reference. Thus, these appeals by special leave.[3]

2. Shri Javali, learned senior counsel for the appellants, contended that since admittedly the partnership firm was not registered as required under Section 69 of the Partnership Act, 1932, the respondent was not entitled to the reference under Section 20 of the Act to an arbitration. He also contended that even assuming that the Court has such power of making reference, it would be only within the parameters of the provisions in Sub-section (3) of Section 69 of the Partnership Act and no other claim is referable for arbitration. He placed strong reliance on Jagdish Chander Gupta v. Kajaria Traders (India) Ltd., MANU/SC/0047/1964 : [1964]8SCR50 , in particular the last paragraph thereof, overruling the Judgment of the Patna High Court in Mahender v. Gum Dayal, AIR (1951) Pat 196. The respondent resisted the contention and relied on Prem Lata v. Ishar Dass Chaman Lal, MANU/SC/0139/1995 : [1995]1SCR168 .[4]

Held, while allowing the appeal:

1. The question then is: what are the items that would be referable to the arbitration? The respondent sought reference of the items mentioned below :[9]

(1) taking out the true and correct account of the profit and loss of account of the profit and loss of erstwhile firm with the help of competent person and carve out the share of the petitioner as per the agreement of partnership deed dated 6.10.1973;

(2) if the respondents are willing to continue the firm in the name and style of the erstwhile firm namely Sri Krishna Motor Service, without taking the petitioner as partner, the quantum of goodwill and compensation payable to the petitioner, as out going partner;

(3) to decide in respect of the vehicle bearing No. MYS5676 and to deliver that vehicle to the petitioner, with reasonable compensation for the use of the said vehicle; and

(4) to find out the changes made in the accounts and the transactions carried out in the name of the erstwhile firm after the dissolution of the firm by notice dated 10.5.1984 to determine the profit and loss of the petitioner or such other reliefs that the Court may deem fit in the circumstances of the case.

2. It would be seen that item (1) clearly falls within the exception provided in Section 69(3). In respect of items (2), though it is widely worded, the respondent would be entitled to the question of entitlement towards the goodwill only upto the date of dissolution of the firm but not thereafter. With regard to items (3) and (4), they arise from the contract and these items would not come under any exceptions engrafted under Section 69(3) of the Partnership Act. Under these circumstances, the High Court was not right in making the reference in item No. (4).[10]

3. The appeals are accordingly allowed to the above extent, but, in the circumstances, without costs. [11]

CHAPTER THIRTEEN

Sharad Vasant Kotak and Ors. vs. Ramniklal Mohanlal Chawda and Ors. (17.12.1997 – SC) : MANU/SC/0910/1998

Relative Section:

Indian Partnership Act, 1932 - Section 17, Section 17(a), Section 30,Section 31,Section 32, Section 4, Section 42, Section 58, Section 59, Section 60, Section 61, Section 62, Section 63, Section 63(1), Section 63(1A), Section 69, Section 69(2), Section 69(2A), Section 69(3)(a), Section 70

Hon'bleJudges/Coram:

S.C. Sen and K. Venkataswami, JJ.

Equivalent Citation: AIR1998SC877, 1998(2)ALLMR(SC)57, 1998(100(1))BOMLR289, 1998 (1) CCC 1 , JT1997(10)SC174, 1998(1)MhLJ372(SC), 1998(1)RCR(Civil)344, 1997(7)SCALE640, (1998)2SCC171, [1997]Supp6SCR543

NumberofPagesintheOriginalJudgment:17

Case Reference:

Madho Prasad v. Gouri Dutt Ganesh Lal MANU/BH/0212/1939; Meenakshi Achi v. P.S.M. Subramanian Chettiar and Ors. MANU/TN/0065/ 1957 Gouri Sankar Sheroff and Ors. v. Central Hindusthan Bank Ltd. and Ors. MANU/WB/0066/1959; CIT v. A.W. Figgis & Co. and Ors. MANU/ SC/0042/1953; Wazid Ali Abid Ali v. CIT MANU/SC/0376/1987; Tyresoles (India) v. CIT MANU/TN/0541/1962; Firm Girdhar Mal Kapur Chand v. Dev Raj Madan Gopal MANU/SC/0015/1963; Pratapchand

Ramchand & Co. v. Jehangirji Bomanji Chinoy MANU/MH/0006/1940; Tapendra Chwider Goopta v. Jogendra Chunder Goopta and Ors. MANU/ WB/0124/1941; Durga Das Janak Raj v. Preete Shah Sant Ram MANU/ PH/0163/1959; Bharat Sarvodaya Mills Co. Ltd. v. Mohatta Bros. MANU/ GJ/0042/1969; Kesrimal and Anr. v. Dalichand and Ors. MANU/RH/0054/ 1959; Maddi Sudarsanam and Ors. v. Borogu Viswanadham Bros. MANU/ AP/0044/1955; CIT v. Pigot Champan & Co. MANU/SC/0137/1982; Nandlal Sohanlal v. CIT MANU/PH/0052/1977

Case Note:

Commercial - registration of partnership firm - Section 69 (2-A) of Partnership Act, 1932 - existing firm reconstituted on induction of new partners - no necessity to get fresh registration - certain penalties provided in Act of 1932 for non-compliance of mandatory provisions in not informing Registrar of Firms about change in Constitution of firm - non-compliance of provisions in respect of giving information to Registrar about changes would not lead to conclusion that firm ceased to exist provisions of Section 69(2-A) not applicable in such case.

Facts:

1. This appeal by special leave has arisen under the following circumstances :-'

2The appellants are the partners of a suit firm called 'M/s. Paramount Builders'. The partnership was entered into on 29.11.1979 with the following individuals as partners :[3]

3. The said partnership firm was registered on 15.12.1980 under Registration No. 158675 with the Registrar of Firms. On 6.5.1986, Shri Mohanlal Hinji Chawda, a partner of the firm (Sr. No. 6 above) died and in his place, his widow Smt. Jijiben Mohanlal Chawda was admitted as a partner in the firm. After the admission of the said Smt. Jijiben Mohanlal Chawda, another deed of partnership was made consisting of the old six partners and the newly admitted partner Smt. Jijiben Mohanlal Chawda. As a matter of fact, the induction of the new partner was not brought to the notice of the Registrar of Firms by forwarding the required particulars. It is on record that still later on 3.11.1992 another partnership deed was brought into existence consisting of the same partners. It is also on record that yet another partner Smt. Hemkuver B. Kotak (S. No. 4 above) died in September, 1994. The fact of death of this partner also was not intimated to the Registrar of Firms. While so, the 1st respondent gave a notice of dissolution of the firm to the appellants and also filed a suit for the

dissolution of the partnership firm bearing suit No. 5016/94 on 15.12.94 in the High Court of Judicature at Bombay on the original side. Initially in the plaint, the constitutional validity of Section 69(2A) of the Indian Partnership Act (hereinafter called the "Act"), as amended by Maharashtra Act, was not raised. The 1st respondent moved a Chamber Summon No. 301/97 seeking permission of the Court to carry out certain amendments to the plaint. Briefly, the amendments sought were that subsequent changes and/or modifications in the partnership deed of M/s. Paramount Builders under the deed of partnership dated 20.10.1986 and also in the deed of partnership dated 3.11.1992 are merely in the nature of changes and/or modifications which do not affect registration of the said firm of M/s. Paramount Builders, as required under the Act, for entitling a partner to institute a suit for reliefs against the partners on dissolution of firms and alternatively, the other amendment sought was to challenge the vires of Section 69(2A) of the Act as in force in the State of Maharashtra.[4]

4. The amendment sought was seriously opposed by the appellants inter alia contending that the suit as filed was not maintainable and, therefore, the amendment cannot be allowed. In other words, according to the appellants on and from 20.10.1986 when a new partnership deed was made, the registration already given to the firm ceased to have validity and the partnership as at present must be deemed to be an unregistered one and, therefore, the suit was hit by Section 69(2A). It was also contended that without impleading State of Maharashtra and Union of India, the vires of Section 69(2A) in the Partnership Act cannot be challenged. The learned trial Judge accepting the objections raised by the appellants found that Section 69(2A) of the Act creates a bar on the threshold of the filing of the suit for the relief covered in the suit and the very suit filed by the plaintiff was incompetent. That being the position, the application for amendment could not be permitted. Consequently, the application was rejected.[5]

5. Aggrieved by the rejection of the amendment application, the first respondent preferred an appeal to the Division Bench of the High Court in Appeal No. 509/97.[6]

6. Ultimately the appellate court allowed the appeal and permitted the amendment only regarding the factual portions and not regarding the constitutional validity of Section 69(2A).[8]

Held, while allowing the appeal:

1. We are also not impressed by the arguments of the learned counsel for the appellants that if the definition of Section 4 is applied to Section

69(2A) then unless the names of all the partners find a place in the Register of Firm, the suit filed by the Plaintiff cannot be sustained. The fact that the firm was registered and Plaintiffs name finds a place in the Register of Firms are not in dispute. The name of the newly introduced partner, of course, does not find a place in the Register of Firms. That means the person whose name does not find a place in the Register of Firms may incur certain disabilities and that will not disable the Plaintiff to press the suit against the firm, which was registered against the persons whose names find a place in the Register of Firms. We are not called upon to decide what are the disabilities of the person, whose name does not find a place in the Register of Firms. For the purpose of Section 69(2A), the partnership firm will mean the firm as found in the certificate of registration and the partners as found in the register of firms maintained as per rule in Form 'G'. The present suit being one for dissolution and accounts by one of the partners, whose name admittedly finds place in the Register of Firms alongwith the names of all the appellants, the requirements of Section 69(2A) are satisfied. Section 4 of the Act is also complied with for this limited purpose.[38]

2. Our conclusion is that on the induction of the second respondent,' the existing firm was only reconstituted on the facts of this case and, therefore, there is no necessity to get a fresh registration. If by virtue of non-compliance of certain mandatory provisions in not informing the Registrar of Firms about the change in the Constitution of the firm, certain penalties provided in the Act alone are attracted and that will not lead to the conclusion that the registration of the firm ceased. This conclusion is based on a conjoint reading of Sections 58-63 and the Forms prescribed thereunder. Further, this conclusion does not in any way militate the object of the Maharashtra Amendment introduced by Act 29 of 84.[39]

3. In the result, we hold that the suit in question is not hit by Section 69(2A) of the Act and, therefore, the Division Bench is right in allowing the Appeal. Consequently, the Appeal is dismissed. However, there will be no order as to costs.

Raptakos Brett and Co. vs. Ganesh Property (09.09.1998 - SC) : MANU/SC/2253/1998

Relative Section:

Transfer of Property Act, 1882 - Section 4, Transfer of Property Act, 1882 - Section 5(1), Transfer of Property Act, 1882 - Section 111(a), Transfer of Property Act, 1882 - Section 108, Transfer of Property Act, 1882 - Section 108(q), Transfer of Property Act, 1882 - Section 116, Transfer of Property Act, 1882 - Section 111; Indian Partnership Act, 1932 - Section 56, Indian Partnership Act, 1932 - Section 57, Indian Partnership Act, 1932 - Section 58, Indian Partnership Act, 1932 - Section 59, Indian Partnership Act, 1932 - Section 69, Indian Partnership Act, 1932 - Section 69(2), Indian Partnership Act, 1932 - Section 69(3); West Bengal Rent Act; Indian Arbitration Act, 1940 - Section 8(2); Karnataka Cinemas (Regulation) Act, 1964; Karnataka Cinemas (Regulation) Rules, 1971 - Rule 6; Indian Railways Act, 1989 - Section 77; Indian Contract Act, 1972; Indian Contract Act, 1872 - Section 1; Limitation Act - Section 14; Companies Act, 1913 - Section 171; Code of Civil Procedure, 1908 (CPC) - Section 80; Code of Civil Procedure, 1908 (CPC) - Order 7 Rule 11, Code of Civil Procedure, 1908 (CPC) - Order 7 Rule 11(d), Code of Civil Procedure, 1908 (CPC) - Order 7 Rule 13, Code of Civil Procedure, 1908 (CPC) - Order 23 Rule 1(3), Code of Civil Procedure, 1908 (CPC) - Order 40 Rule 1; Rent Restriction Act

Hon'bleJudges/Coram:

S.B. Majmudar and M. Jagannadha Rao, JJ.
Equivalent Citation: 1998(2)ARC710, 1998 (4) CCC 1
NumberofPagesintheOriginalJudgment: 24
Case Reference:
Udhav Singh v. Madhav Rao Scindia MANU/SC/0302/1975 : 1976 (2)
SCR 246; Ram Sarup Gupta (Dead) by LRs. v. Bishun Narain Inter College
and Ors. MANU/SC/0043/1987 : 1987 (2) SCC 555; Jagdish Chander Gupta
v. Kajaria Traders (India) Ltd. MANU/SC/0047/1964 : 1964 (8) SCR 50;
Ganga Dutt Murarka v. Kartik Chandra Das and Ors. MANU/SC/0347/1961
: 1961 (3) SCR 813; M.C. Chockalingam and Ors. v. V. Manickavasagam
and Ors. MANU/SC/0338/1973 : 1974 (1) SCC 48; R.V. Bhupal Prasad v.
State of A.P. and Ors. MANU/SC/0035/1996 : 1995 (5) SCC 698 : 1996
SCFBRC 29 (SC); Smt. Shanti Devi v. Amal Kumar Banerjee MANU/SC/
0536/1981 : 1981 (2) SCC 199; Murlidhar Jalan (since deceased) through
his LRs. v. State of Meghalaya and Ors. MANU/SC/0720/1997 : 1997 (5)
SCC 480; D.H. Maniar and Ors. v. Waman Laxman Kudav MANU/SC/
0350/1976 : 1977 (1) SCR 403; Sivjnanam Abraham and Ors. v. Mathevan
Pillai Bhoothalingam Pillai and Ors. AIR 1952 Vol. 39 Travancore 359; Mrs.
Thayarammal v. People's Charity Fund, Bangalore and Ors. MANU/KA/
0140/1978 : AIR 1978 Karnataka 125; Henderson v. Squire 1869 LR 4 QB
170; Venkatesh Narayan v. Krishnaji Arjun 8 Bom. 160; M/s. Goraknath
Champalal Pandey v. Hansraj Manot MANU/WB/0364/1969 : Calcutta
Weekly Notes Vol. 74 (1969-79) 269; Hansraj Manot v. M/s. Goraknath
Champalal Pandey MANU/WB/0357/1961 : Calcutta Weekly Notes, Vol.
66 (1961-62) 262; Padam Singh Jain v. M/s. Chandra Brothers and Ors.
MANU/BH/0014/1990 : AIR 1990 Patna 95; Madan Lal v. Bhai Anand
Singh and Ors. MANU/SC/0619/1972 : 1973 (1) SCC 84; M/s. Jammu Cold
Storage and General Mills Ltd. v. M/s. Khairati Lal and Sons MANU/JK/
0040/1960 : AIR 1960 Jammu & Kashmir 101; Danmal Parshotam Dass
(Firm) v. Babu Ram-Chhote Lal (Firm) MANU/UP/0139/1935 : AIR 1936
Allahabad 3; Dwijendra Nath Singh and Anr. v. Govinda Chandra and Anr.
MANU/WB/0186/1953 : AIR 1953 Calcutta 497; The Commissioner of
Income Tax, Andhra Pradesh, Hyderabad v. M/s. Jayalakshmi Rice and
Oil Mills Contractor Co. MANU/SC/0409/1971 : 1971 (1) SCC 280; M/s.
Shreeram Finance Corporation v. Yasin Khan and Ors. MANU/SC/0341/
1989 : 1989 (3) SCC 476; Sunderlal and Sons v. Yagendra Nath Singh and
Anr. MANU/WB/0090/1976 : AIR 1976 Calcutta 471; Jakiuddin Badruddin
and Ors. v. Vithoba Jagannath Gadali and Anr. MANU/NA/0144/1939 : AIR

1939 Nagpur 301; Nazir Ahmad and Ors. v. Peoples Bank of Northern India Ltd. (in liquidation) through Official Liquidator and Ors. MANU/LA/0059/1942 : AIR 29 (1942) Lahore 289; Abdul Karim v. Ramdas Narayandas Shop MANU/NA/0017/1950 : ILR 1951 Nagpur 31; Des Raj Prem Chand and Anr. (Firm) v. Hira Lal Kali Ram and Anr. (Firm) MANU/PH/0177/1952 : AIR 1952 Punjab 415; Puran Mal Ganga Ram (Firm) v. The Central Bank of India Ltd. MANU/PH/0096/1953 : AIR 1953 Punjab 235; Smt. Saiyada Mossarrat v. Hindustan Steel Ltd., Bhilai Steel Plant, Bhilai (MP) and Ors. MANU/SC/0454/1988 : 1989 (1) SCC 272; The Mumbai Kamgar Sabha, Bombay v. M/s. Abdulbhai Faizullabhai and Ors. MANU/SC/0313/1976 : 1976 (3) SCC 832; Sreenivasa General Traders and Ors. v. State of Andhra Pradesh and Ors. MANU/SC/0278/1983 : 1983 (4) SCC 353; Bansidhar Sankarlal v. Md. Ibrahim and Anr. MANU/SC/0506/1970 : AIR 1971 SC 1292; Everest Coal Company Pvt. Ltd. v. State of Bihar and Ors. MANU/SC/0009/1977 : AIR 1977 SC 2304

Case Note:

Civil - Suit for possession and damages for illegal occupation - Whether the suit filed by the Respondent was barred under Section 69(2) of the Partnership Act either wholly or in part and if the suit was so barred, whether subsequent registration of the Plaintiff's firm under the Partnership Act could revive the suit to make it competent at least from the date on which such registration pending the suit was obtained by the Respondent firm?

Facts:

The Respondent-Plaintiff was the owner of suit premises. The said premises was rented to the Appellant-Defendant on a monthly rent by a registered lease for a period of 21 years. On the expiry of the said period, the Respondent-Plaintiff alleging to be a registered partnership firm, filed the aforesaid suit praying for a decree for possession as well as damages for illegal occupation of the premises by the Appellant-Defendant. The defence of the Appellant-Defendant was that after the expiry of the lease period, it had continued to be a tenant by acceptance of rent by the Defendant-landlord and hence it had become a tenant by holding over Under Section 116 of the Transfer of Property Act, 1882 (Property Act). Further defence was taken by the Appellant-Defendant by way of a separate application seeking dismissal of the suit under Order VII, Rule 11(d) of Code of Civil Procedure (CPC) on the ground that the suit for possession as filed by the Plaintiff-Respondent, which was an unregistered partnership firm, was not maintainable.

Held while dismissing the appeal:

(i) On the expiry of the period of lease, the erstwhile lessee continues in possession because of the law of the land, namely that the original landlord cannot physically throw out such an erstwhile tenant by force. He must get his claim for possession adjudicated by a competent Court as per the relevant provisions of law. The status of an erstwhile tenant has to be treated as a tenant at sufferance akin to a trespasser having no independent right to continue in possession. [18]

(ii). The plaint as framed by the Plaintiff Respondent was base on a composite cause of action consisting of two parts. One part referred to the breach of the covenant on the part of the Defendant when it failed to deliver vacant possession to the Plaintiff lessor on the expiry of the lease and thereafter all throughout and thus it was guilty of breach of relevant covenants of the lease. The second part of the cause of action, however, was based on the statutory obligation of the Defendant lessee when it failed to comply with its statutory obligation Under Section 108(q) read with Section 111(a) of the Property Act. So far as this second part of the cause of action is concerned it could not certainly be said that it was arising out of the erstwhile contract. [27]

(iii) There is no further locus poenitentiae given to the tenant to continue to remain in possession after the determination of lease by efflux of time on the basis of any such contrary express term in the lease. Consequently, it was the legal obligation flowing from Section 108(q) of the Act which would get squarely attracted on the facts of the present case and once this suit was also for enforcement of such a legal right under the law of the land available to the landlord it could not be said that enforcement of such right arose out of any of the express terms of the contract which would in turn get visited by the bar of Section 69, Sub-section (2) of the Partnership Act. Enforcement of that right had nothing to do with the earlier contract which had stood determined by efflux of time. The first point for determination, was accordingly held partly in favour of the Plaintiff and partly in favour of the Defendant. As the decree for possession was passed on the basis of both parts of causes of action, even if it was not supportable on the first part, it would remain well sustained on the second part of the very same cause of action.[28]

Disposition: Appeal Dismissed

• 64 •

Laxmidas Dahyabhai Kabarwala vs. Nanabhai Chunilal Kabarwala and Ors. (27.03.1963 - SC) : MANU/ SC/0019/1963

Relative Section:

Constitution Of India - Article 136; Indian Partnership Act, 1932 - Section 37, Indian Partnership Act, 1932 - Section 55(1), Indian Partnership Act, 1932 - Section 69(3)(a); Limitation Act, 1963 - Section 3

Hon'bleJudges/Coram:

A.K. Sarkar, N. Rajagopala Ayyangar and S.K. Das, JJ.

Equivalent Citation: AIR1964SC11, [1964]2SCR567

NumberofPagesintheOriginalJudgment: 15

Case Reference:

(Mian) Pir Bux vs. Mohomed Tahar MANU/PR/0045/1934; Currimbhoy and Company, Limited vs. Creet MANU/PR/0066/1932

Case Note:

Commercial - counter claim - Order 6 Rule 17 and Order 8 Rule 6 of Code of civil Procedure, 1908, Section 37 of Partnership Act, 1932, Article 136 of Constitution of India and Section 34 of Arbitration Act - firm commenced by plaintiff and widow of deceased partner - winding up of firm sought - oral agreement entered for distribution of property of firm - respondents denied agreement after death of widow - counter claim filed seeking ascertainment of claim and cost - suit filed by appellant - respondent filed written statement denying statement - respondent had no right to have their counter claim treated as plaint - respondent to file suit to enforce subject matter of counter claim - when Court directs counter claim to be treated as plaint then date of presentation of plaint is date of Court's Order - Court has no power to extend period of limitation - no question of amendment when Court orders claim to be treated as plaint - respondent claimed that they filed written statement and not plaint - no plaint was filed - no question of curing any irregularities in filing of plaint arise.

Facts:

The plaintiff, who is the appellant before us, and one Jamnadas Ghelabhai were partners in a business commenced in October 1913 and carried on under the name and style of Bharat Medical Stores at Broach, the two partners having equal shares. During the subsistence of the partnership and from and out of the assets thereof an immovable property - a house was purchased at Broach in July 1932. Jamnadas Ghelabhai died on August 12, 1943 but the partnership business was continued thereafter by the plaintiff-appellant taking in Bai Itcha - the widow of the deceased partner - in his place. A change was, however, made in the shares of the two partners, in that Bai Itcha was given only a $1/4^{th}$ share as against the $1/2$ share enjoyed by her husband. With this alteration the same business was carried on between the two partners. In the early part of 1950 Bai Itcha fell ill. It was the case of the plaintiff that there were negotiations between the two partners as regards the winding up of the firm and it was his further case that on July 9, 1950 two matters were the subject of a concluded agreement with her. These were (1) that the partnership would stand dissolved from July 15, 1950 and that Bai Itcha would receive from the plaintiff a sum of Rs. 13,689/- in full satisfaction in respect of the capital contributed by her as well as for her share of the profits of the firm, (2) that the plaintiff was to take over the immovable property in Broach purchased by the firm in July 1932 for its book value and that he should on that account pay over to Bai Itcha Rs. 2,202/9/9 being a moiety of the book value. The agreement was stated to be wholly oral and was admittedly not reduced to writing. Before, however, anything was done in pursuance of the alleged arrangement, Bai Itcha died on July 31, 1950 leaving as her heirs the respondents who were the sons of a brother of Jamnadas Ghelabhai - Bai Itcha's husband. It was the further case of the appellant that after the death of Bai Itcha respondents 1 and 2 examined the accounts of the partnership and after satisfying themselves that Rs. 13,689/- was the proper figure of the sum due to the deceased partner agreed to receive the same in full satisfaction of the amount to which they were entitled in respect of that item. All these allegations about the agreement with Bai Itcha and the confirmation by them of the said agreement after her death were, however, denied by the respondents who insisted upon their rights under the law as legal representatives of the deceased partner.

Held, while allowing the appeal:

43. Neither does it seem to me that the order can be treated as one curing an irregularity; as a case where the counter-claim had been a plaint from the beginning but as it had not complied with the rules concerning a plaint it had been a plaint irregularly filed. First, the respondents never contended that they had filed a plaint. They said, they had filed a written statement in which they had made a counter-claim and that counter-claim was maintainable as such. That was their contention. They persisted in this attitude all through. They did not even raise an issue as to whether they were entitled to treat the counter-claim as a plaint. It would be strange if the Court said that the respondents had filed a plaint though they did not themselves say so. Secondly, I am not aware that a plaint and a written statement can be combined in one pleading so that the filing of the one is the filing of the other. This is impossible under our procedure. It must be taken that what had originally been filed was a written statement, and, therefore, that no plaint had at all been filed. If no plaint had been filed, no question of curing any irregularity in the filing of a plaint can arise.[43]

44. For these reasons I would allow the appeal with costs here and in the High Court.[44]

45. BY COURT : In accordance with the majority opinion the appeal is dismissed with costs subject to the directions contained in the judgment.[45]

Appeal dismissed.

CHAPTER SIXTEEN

Jagdish Chander Gupta vs. Kajaria Traders (India) Ltd. (29.04.1964 - SC) : MANU/ SC/0047/1964

Relative Section:

Arbitration Act, 1940 [repealed] - Section 8, Arbitration Act, 1940 [repealed] - Section 8(2); Indian Partnership Act, 1932 - Section 56, Indian Partnership Act, 1932 - Section 69, Indian Partnership Act, 1932 - Section 69(3); Presidency Small Cause Courts Act, 1882 - Section 19

Hon'bleJudges/Coram:

K.C. Das Gupta, K.N. Wanchoo, M. Hidayatullah and N. Rajagopala Ayyangar, JJ.

Equivalent Citation: Babulal Dhandhania vs. Gauttam and Co. MANU/ WB/0145/1950

NumberofPagesintheOriginalJudgment: 6

Case Reference: Babulal Dhandhania vs. Gauttam and Co. MANU/WB/ 0145/1950

Case Note:

Constitution - unregistered firm - Section 69 of Indian Partnership Act, 1932 and Section 8 (2) of Arbitration Act, 1940 - appellant and respondent are partners in unregistered partnership firm - partnership agreement includes arbitration clause - respondent made application to Court under Section 8 (2) to appoint arbitrator to settle dispute - appellant challenged application on ground that Section 8 (2) not applicable and application barred by Section 69 - High Court decided that Section 8 (2) applicable and Section 69 does not bar application - decision challenged only on ground that Section 69 bars application under Section 8 (2) - Supreme Court observed Section 69 bars certain proceedings including proceedings to enforce right arising from contract as consequence of non registration of firms - application to Court under Section 8 (2) amounts to right arising from contract - Supreme Court held, application under Section 8 (2) cannot be made.

Facts:

1. This appeal by special leave is directed against an order of the High Court of Bombay dated March 22, 1960 in its ordinary original civil jurisdiction. The facts are simple. By a letter dated July 30, 1955, Messrs. Kajaria Traders (India) Ltd., who is the respondent here and Messrs. Foreign Import and Export Association (sole proprietary firm owned by the appellant Jagdish C. Gupta) entered into a partnership to export between January and June 1956, 10,000 tons of manganese ore to Phillips Brothers (India) Ltd., New York. Each partner was to supply a certain quantity of manganese ore. We are not concerned with the terms of the agreement but with one of its clauses which provided :

"That in case of dispute the matter will be referred for arbitration in accordance with the Indian Arbitration Act."

2. The company alleged that Jagdish Chander Gupta failed to carry out his part of the partnership agreement. After some correspondence, the company wrote to Jagdish Chander Gupta on February 28, 1959 that they had appointed Mr. R. J. Kolah (Advocate O.S.) as their arbitrator and asked Jagdish Chander Gupta either to agree to Mr. Kolah's appointment as sole arbitrator or to appoint his own arbitrator. Jagdish Chander Gupta put off consideration and on March 17, 1959 the company informed Jagdish Chander Gupta that as he failed to appoint an arbitrator within 15 clear days they were appointing Mr. Kolah as sole arbitrator. Jagdish Chander Gupta disputed this and the company filed on March 28, 1959 an application under s. 8(2) of the Indian Arbitration Act, 1940 for the appointment of Mr. Kolah or any other person as arbitrator.

3. Jagdish Chander Gupta appeared and objected inter alia to the institution of the petition. Two grounds were urged (i) that s. 8(2) of the Indian Arbitration Act was not applicable as it was not expressly provided in the arbitration clause quoted above that the arbitrators were to be by consent of the parties and (ii) that s. 69(3) of the Indian Partnership Act, 1932 afforded a bar to the petition because the partnership was not

registered. The petition was referred by the Chief Justice to a Divisional Bench consisting of Mr. Justice Mudholkar (as he then was) and Mr. Justice Naik. The two learned Judges agreed that in the circumstances of the case an application under s. 8 of the Indian Arbitration Act was competent and that the court had power to appoint an arbitrator. They disagreed on the second point : Mr. Justice Mudholkar was of the opinion that s. 69(3) of the Indian Partnership Act barred the application while Mr. Justice Naik held otherwise. The case was then referred to Mr. Justice K. T. Desai (as he then was) and he agreed with Mr. Justice Naik with the result that the application was held to be competent.

Held, while allowing the appeal:

1. In our judgment, the words 'other proceeding' in sub-s. (3) must receive their full meaning untrammeled by the words 'a claim of set-off'. The latter words neither intend nor can be construed to cut down the generality of the words 'other proceeding'. The sub-section provides for the application of the provisions of sub-ss. (1) and (2) to claims of set-off and also to other proceedings of any kind which can properly be said to be for enforcement of any right arising from contract except those expressly mentioned as exceptions in sub-s. (3) and sub s. (4).[11]

2. The appeal is, therefore, allowed. The decision of the High Court will be set aside and the application under s. 8(2) of the Arbitration Act shall stand dismissed with costs throughout on the applicant in the High Court.[12]

3. Appeal allowed. [13]

CHAPTER SEVENTEEN

Commissioner of Income Tax, Madras vs. R.M. Chidambaram Pillai and Ors. (17.11.1976 - SC) : MANU/SC/ 0217/1976

Relative Section:

General Clauses Act 1897 - Section 3(42); Income Tax Act, 1961 - Section 10, Income Tax Act, 1961 - Section 10(1), Income Tax Act, 1961 - Section 10(2), Income Tax Act, 1961 - Section 10(4), Income Tax Act, 1961 - Section 10(4)(b), Income Tax Act, 1961 - Section 16, Income Tax Act, 1961 - Section 16(1)(b), Income Tax Act, 1961 - Section 24; Indian Partnership Act, 1932 - Section 13, Indian Partnership Act, 1932 - Section 2(6B), Indian Partnership Act, 1932 - Section 3, Indian Partnership Act, 1932 - Section 4

Hon'bleJudges/Coram:

H.R. Khanna and V.R. Krishna Iyer, JJ.

Equivalent Citation: AIR1977SC489, [1977]106ITR292(SC), (1977)1SCC431, 1977SCC(Tax)188, [1977] 2SCR111

NumberofPagesintheOriginalJudgment:9

Case Reference:

Mathew Abraham v. Commissioner of Income tax MANU/TN/0578/ 1962; R.M. Chidambaram Pillai v. Commissioner of Income tax MANU/ TN/0213/1970

Case Note:

Direct Taxation - taxable income - Sections 3, 4 and 13 of Partnership Act - respondent-partners carrying on business of tea which is largely agricultural and partly non-agricultural - partners were entitled to draw salary in addition to profits - whether any portion of salaries so drawn by partners for services they rendered are agricultural income to be non-exigible to income tax - 40% of income from tea sales is treated as taxable - 60% regarded as agricultural and exempt from taxation - partner cannot be employed by his firm as a man cannot be his own employer - salaries are profits known by different name - salaries drawn by partners are taxable as profits by business in firm.

Facts:

1. A fine point of law, which lends itself to subtle spinning of gossamer webs of argument, falls for decision in these appeals by certificate. Were the policy of the law been plain, the language should have been clearer and the labours of courts could have been lesser. The arguments have been exhaustive, the precedents, in profusion, cited to the point of no return and the short issue expanded into learned length; but, at the end of the forensic journey, we are hesitantly inclined to leave the judgment under appeal undisturbed as the law set out therein has better appeal and theoretical soundness than the rival view point well-presented by Sri Ahuja for the appellant (Revenue). The planning and pruning of case law is perhaps necessary if time-consuming court proceedings are to be curbed. 'All our life is crushed by the weight of words : the weight of the dead', said Luigi Pirandello. Heavy case-law must not clog judicial navigation.

2. Next to a abbreviate statement of the facts which project the legal issue canvassed before us. Two tea estates were owned by two firms with several partners, two of whom were the respondents, in the two sets of appeals. C.As. 17 to 19 and C.As. 20 and 21 of 1972. The tea sold yielded income composite in character, being largely agricultural and partly non-agricultural. The complex situation of apportionment between the two heads for purposes of income-tax has been taken care of by Rule 24 of the Income-tax Rules, both the firms having been registered under the Act.

Held, while allowing the appeal:

1. We regard this conclusion as unsound, the source of the error being a failure to appreciate that the salary of a partner is but an alias for the return, by way of profits, for the human capital sweat, skill and toil are. in our socialist republic, productive investment he has brought in for common

benefit. The immediate reason for payment of salary was service contract but the causa causans is partnership.[25]

2. We dismiss the appeals. When this Court, as the apex adjudicator declaring the law for the country and invested with constitutional credentials under Article 141, clarifies a confused juridical situation, its substantial role is of legal mentor of the nation. Such is the spirit of the ruling in Trustees of Port, Bombay MANU/SC/0402/1974 : [1974]3SCR397 . If parties have been fair, the costs of the litigation must come out of the national exchequer, not out of a party's purse. We direct both sides to bear their costs throughout.[26]

CHAPTER EIGHTEEN

Badri Prasad and Ors. vs. Nagarmal and Ors. (09.12.1958 - SC) : MANU/SC/0009/1958

Relative Section:

Companies Act, 1956 - Section 4; Indian Contract Act, 1872 - Section 72; Indian Partnership Act, 1932 - Section 69(3)(a); Indian Stamp Act, 1899 - Section 7

Hon'bleJudges/Coram:

J.L. Kapur, S.K. Das and Syed Jaffer Imam, JJ.

Equivalent Citation: AIR1959SC559, 1959(1)CLJ205, [1959]29CompCas229(SC), 1959Supp(1)SCC769, [1959]Supp1SCR769

NumberofPagesintheOriginalJudgment:6

Case Reference: nil

Case Note:

Rewa Companies Act, 1955, s.4(2)

Indian Partnership Act, 1932, s.69(3)(a)

Maintainability of Suit-Company unregistered-Suit by members for accounts-New point.

Facts:

1. This is an appeal on a certificate granted by the erstwhile Judicial Commissioner of Vindhya Pradesh, which is now part of the State of Madhya Pradesh. On behalf of respondent no. 1, Nagar Mal, who was defendant no. 1 in the suit, a preliminary objection has been taken to the effect that the suit was not maintainable by reason of the provisions of

section 4 of the Rewa State Companies Act, 1935, and the appeal filed by the plaintiffs must, therefore, be dismissed. As this preliminary objection was not taken in any of the two courts below, learned counsel for the appellants wanted time to consider the point. Accordingly, on October 28, 1958, we adjourned the hearing of the appeal for about a month. The appeal was then heard on November 27, 1958.

2. As we are of the opinion that the preliminary objection must succeed, it is necessary to state the facts only in so far as they have a bearing on it. When cloth control came into force in Rewa State, the cloth dealers of Budhar a town in that State, formed themselves into an Association to collect the quota of cloth to be allotted to them and sell it on profit wholesale and retail. The Association at Budhar consisted of 25 members who made contributions to the initial capital of the association which was one lac of rupees. No formal Articles of Association were written; nor was it registered. The Association functioned through a President and a pioneer worker; they kept accounts and distributed the profits. Respondent no. 1, Nagar Mal, was the President of the said Association from January 1946 to June 26, 1946. Before that, Seth Badri Prasad, one of the plaintiffs-appellants before us, was the President. Nagar Mal ceased to be President after June 26, 1946, and Seth Badri Prasad again became President. The Association worked till February 1948; then cloth was decontrolled and the work of the Association came to an end. On June 25, 1949, thirteen members of the Association out of the twenty-five brought a suit, and in the plaint they alleged that respondent no. 1, who was President of the Association, from January 1946 to June 1946, had given an account of income and expenditure for the months of January, February and March, 1946, but had given no accounts for the months of April, May and June, 1946

3. Besides Nagar Mal the other eleven businessmen, who we members of the Association, were joined as proforma defendants, some of whom later filed an application to be joined as plaintiffs. Though the plaint did not mention any particular transaction of the Association during the period when Nagar Mal was its President, the judgments of the courts below show that the real dispute between the parties related to the sale of cloth of a consignment known as the Gwalior consignment. It appears that in April 1946 a consignment of 666 bales of cloth had come from Gwalior and an order was passed by the Cloth Control Officer that the consignment would be allotted to Nagar Mal who would give the Association an option

of taking over the consignment; if the Association did not exercise the option, the consignment would be taken over by Nagar Mal. It appears that there was some dispute as to whether the other members of the Association were willing to take over the consignment of Gwalior cloth. We are not concerned now with the details of that dispute because we are not deciding the appeal on merits. It is enough if we say that ultimately there was an order to the effect that only 390 bales should be allotted to the Association out of which Nagar Mal had given the Association benefit of the sales of 106 bales, and the dispute related to the share of profits made on the remaining 284 bales.

Held, while allowing the appeal

1. As to the last contention of learned counsel for the appellants, based on the analogy of section 69(3)(a) of the Partnership Act, it is enough to point out that under the Indian partnership Act, 1932, an unregistered firm is not illegal; there is no direct compulsion that a partnership firm must be registered, though the disabilities consequent on non-registration may be extremely inconvenient. Moreover, the suit before us was not one for accounts of a dissolved firm, but for accounts of an illegal association which was in existence at the relevant period for which accounts were asked. We do not think that the argument by analogy is of any help to the appellants; in our opinion, the analogy does not really apply.[15]

2. For the reasons given above, we hold that the preliminary objection succeeds. The appeal is accordingly dismissed. As the preliminary objection was taken at a very late stage, we direct that the parties must bear their own costs of the hearing in this Court.[16]

3. Appeal dismissed.

Karumuthu Thiagarajan Chettiar and Ors. vs. E.M. Muthappa Chettiar (27.02.1961 - SC) : MANU/SC/ 0059/1961

Relative Section:

Indian Partnership Act, 1932 - Section 10, Indian Partnership Act, 1932 - Section 13(f), Indian Partnership Act, 1932 - Section 42, Indian Partnership Act, 1932 - Section 43, Indian Partnership Act, 1932 - Section 44, Indian Partnership Act, 1932 - Section 69, Indian Partnership Act, 1932 - Section 7, Indian Partnership Act, 1932 - Section 8, Indian Partnership Act, 1932 - Section 9

Hon'bleJudges/Coram:

K.N. Wanchoo and P.B. Gajendragadkar, JJ.

Equivalent Citation: AIR1961SC1225, 1962(1)AnWR19, [1962]32CompCas155(SC), (1962)IIMLJ19, [1961]3SCR998

NumberofPagesintheOriginalJudgment:9

Case Reference:

Morarji Goculdas and Co. vs. Sholapur Spinning and Weaving Co. Ltd. and Ors. MANU/PR/0033/1943

Case Note:

Partnership Act, 1932, ss.7,10,13(g)

Partnership-Duration not provided expressly-When it can be implied-Termination of partnership on Notice.

Facts:

1. This is an appeal on a certificate granted by the Madras High Court. The brief facts necessary for present purposes are these : The present suit was brought by Muthappa Chettiar (hereinafter referred to as the respondent) against K. Thiagarajan Chettiar (hereinafter called the appellant) and the Saroja Mills Ltd. In 1939 these two persons thought of doing business jointly by securing managing agencies of some mills. In that connection they carried on negotiations with two mills, namely, Rajendra Mills Limited, Salem and the Saroja Mills Limited, Coimbatore (hereinafter called the Mills). The managing agency of the Mills was with the Cotton Corporation Limited. On October 4, 1939, the said Corporation transferred and assigned its rights to the appellant and the respondent under the name of Muthappa and Co. On November 15, 1939, the Mills at an extra-ordinary general meeting of the shareholders accepted Muthappa and Co. as the managing agents and made the necessary changes in the Articles of Association. Later the appellant and the respondent obtained the managing agency of the Rajendra Mills Limited, Salem. The managing agents of this mill were Salem Balasubramaniam and Co. Ltd. Muthappa and Co. purchased all the shares of the Salem Balasubramaniam and Co. and thereafter carried on the business of the managing agency of this mill in the name of Salem Balasubramaniam and Co. Ltd. In November 1940 the appellant and the respondent entered into a written partnership agreement with respect to the managing agency business of the two mills. We shall consider the terms of this agreement later and all that we need say at this stage is that turns were fixed for the appellant and respondent to look after the actual management of the two mills and the appellant's turn was the first and he therefore came into actual control of the two mills. Soon after however disputes arose between the appellant and the respondent with respect to the managing agency of the Rajendra Mills Limited, which resulted in various suits being filed between the partners, to which we shall refer later. Eventually on March 4, 1943, the appellant gave notice to the respondent terminating the partnership, considering it as a partnership at will. This was followed by the directors of the Mills terminating the managing agency of Muthappa and Co. on the ground that that company had ceased to exist and also on the ground that quarrels between the partners of the firm were not conducive to good management of the Mills. This was

notified to the respondent on March 22, 1943. This action of the directors was approved in a meeting of the shareholders of the Mills on September 29, 1943, and necessary modifications were again made in the Articles of Association. In between on April 17, 1943, the respondent had filed a suit for a declaration that Muthappa and Co. continued to be the managing agents of the Mills and for obtaining possession of the office of managing agents for himself or along with the appellant and also for a permanent injunction restraining the Mills from appointing any other managing agents. This suit was dismissed by the trial court on the ground that it was not maintainable under s. 69 of the Indian Partnership Act, No. IX of 1932 (hereinafter called the Act), though the trial court gave findings on other issues also. The respondent went up in appeal to the Madras High Court against the decree in that suit. This appeal was dismissed on July 8, 1948, as the High Court held that the finding of the subordinate judge that the suit was not maintainable under s. 69 of the Act was correct. The High Court however made it clear that it was expressing no opinion on the correctness or otherwise of the other findings recorded by the subordinate judge.

Held, while allowing the appeal

1. That leaves the question of costs. So far as Saroja Mills Limited are concerned, we are of opinion that they are entitled to their costs throughout from the respondent as their action in terminating the managing agency has been held by us to be legal and valid. As to Thiagarajan Chettiar we are of opinion that in the circumstances of this case, the order of the subordinate judge that Muthappa Chettiar (respondent) and Thiagarajan Chettiar (appellant) should bear their own costs is just and we order them to bear their own costs throughout.[16]

2. We therefore allow the appeal in part and order that accounts will be taken from November 15, 1939, to March 22, 1943, as between Thiagarajan Chettiar and Muthappa Chettiar. The respondent will pay the costs of Saroja Mills Limited throughout; but Muthappa Chettiar and Thiagarajan Chettiar will bear their own costs throughout.[17]

3. Appeal allowed in part.

CHAPTER TWENTY

Commissioner of Income Tax, Bangalore vs. K. D. Kamath and Company. (11.10.1971 - SC) : MANU/SC/0745/1971

Relative Section:

Indian Contract Act, 1872 - Section 27; Section 11, Section 11(1), Section 14, - Section 18, Section 19(1), Section 20, Section 22, Section 6

Hon'bleJudges/Coram:

C.A. Vaidialingam, J.

Equivalent Citation: (1972)1CTR(SC)124

NumberofPagesintheOriginalJudgment: 14

Case Reference: nil

Case Note:

Direct Taxation - Registration - Section 26A of Indian Income-tax Act, 1922 - Appellate Tribunal held that deed did create relationship of partners inter se between parties thereto and directed Income Tax Officer to register firm under Section 26A of Act - Hence, this Appeal - Whether, deed, marked Ex. A was an Instrument of Partnership on basis of which Appellant firm was eligible for registration under Act - Held, management and control of business on behalf of all partners was done by party No. 1 - Under Section 18 of Partnership Act, partner was agent of firm for purpose of business of firm - However, that section itself clearly said that it was subject to provisions of Act - It was open to parties, under section 11, to enter into agreement regarding their mutual rights and duties as partners of firm and that could be done by contract, which in case was evidenced by deed of partnership -- Hence, all ingredients of partnership were satisfied under partnership deed and that view of High Court that Appellant firm could not be granted registration under Section 26A of Income-tax Act for assessment could not be sustained - Appeal allowed.

Ratio Decidendi: "Relationship of partners, which is not been created under deed of partnership before Court, cannot be sustained."

Facts:

1. This appeal, by special leave, raises the question whether the deed dated March 20, 1959 and marked Ex. A is an Instrument of Partnership on the basis of which the appellant firm is eligible to be granted registration under sec. 26A of the Indian Income-tax, Act, 1922 (hereinafter to be referred as the Income-tax Act).

2. The appellant is a firm consisting of six partners and the partnership was constituted under the document dated March 20, 1959. The business of the partnership, as recited in the deed, is stated to have been carried on in partnership was registered under the Indian Partnership Act, 1922, (hereinafter to be referred as the Partnership Act) on or about August 11, 1959. For the assessment year 1959-60, corresponding to the previous year ending March 31, 1959, the appellant filed an application to the Income Tax Officer, A Ward, Dharwar under sec. 26-A for registration of the partnership in the name of M/s K. D. Kamath & Company. The Income Tax Officer by his order dated September 28, 1960 declined to grant registration on the ground that there was no genuine partnership brought into existence by the deed of March 20, 1959 and that the claim of the firm having been constituted is not genuine. The said officer further held that the business should be held to be the sole concern of K. D. Kamath. For coming to this conclusion the Income Tax Officer has mainly relied on clauses 8, 9, 12 and 16 of the Partnership deed. Though the Income Tax Officer has used a loose expression that there is no genuine partnership, the sum and substance of his finding is that there is no relationship of partner inter se created under the position before us by stating that the Department is not challenging the

Held, while allowing the appeal

1. To conclude, we are of the opinion that all the ingredients of partnership are satisfied under the partnership deed dated March 20, 1959 and that the view of the High Court that the appellant firm cannot be granted registration under sec. 26A of the Income-tax act for the assessment year 1959-60 cannot be sustained.[35]

2. In the result, we answer the question of law in the affirmative in favour of the assessee. This answer given by us to the question referred to the

High Court by the Income-tax Appellate Tribunal will be substituted in the place that given by the High Court. We accordingly reverse that judgment and order of the High Court and allow the appeal with costs. [36]

M.O.H. Uduman and Ors. vs. M.O.H. Aslum (13.11.1990 - SC) : MANU/SC/0238/1991

Relative Section:

Constitution Of India - Article 240;

Indian Partnership Act, 1932 - Section 11(1), Section 32(1), Section 40, Indian Partnership Act, 1932 - Section 43, Indian Partnership Act, 1932 - Section 44, Indian Partnership Act, 1932 - Section 69, Section 7.

Hon'bleJudges/Coram:

L.M. Sharma and K. Ramaswamy, JJ.

Equivalent Citation: AIR1991SC1020, 1991 (1) CCC 1 , JT1991(1)SC138, 1990-2-LW642, (1991)IMLJ46(SC), (1991)1SCC412, [1990]Supp2SCR663, 1991(1)UJ203

NumberofPagesintheOriginalJudgment:7

Case Reference:

Banarsi Das vs. Seth Kanshi Ram and Ors. MANU/SC/0302/1962; Karumuthu Thiagarajan Chettiar and Anr. vs. E.M. Muthappa Chettiar MANU/SC/0059/1961

Case Note:

Commercial - duration of partnership - Section 7 of Partnership Act, 1932 - appellant contended that under French law partnership was not at will - Trial Court agreed with contention and held that suit for dissolution of partnership was not maintainable - High Court reversed findings of Trial Court and held that partnership is at will and respondent can seek dissolution - Supreme Court observed that contract of partnership consistent with French Civil Code and may be adjudicated accordingly -

in a contract of partnership intention of parties has to be gathered from languages used by adopting harmonious construction - duration of partnership has been expressly provided under Will and partnership shall continue till there are two partners - respondent has no right to withdraw or retire from partnership or seek dissolution of firm - in case if he so desires he can amend plaint appropriately and seek decree in this regard

Facts:

The appeal arises against the judgment and decree of the Division Bench of the Madras High Court dated November 17, 1988 made in L.P.A. No. 113 of 1986 reversing the judgment and decree of the learned Single Judge and of the First Add. Subordinate Judge, Pondicherry in O.S. No. 206 of 1978. The facts are that the appellants/defendants 1 to 3 and the respondent, plaint: ff are sons of the 4th appellant/defendant-their mother. Their rather, M.O. Hassan Kuthus Marican, started the proprietary concern M/s. M.O. Hassan Tithus Marican doing import and export and other business in Pondicherry. On July 20, 1962, a partnership consisting of the appellants, the respondent and the father, Ex. B1 (a translation copy in English is Ex. B1/a) was constituted and was registered as per the provisions of the French Law and the business was carried on. By relinquishment deed, Ex. B2 dated August 1, 1968 their father had retired from the partnership. Thereafter the appellants and the respondent continued the business in terms of Ex. B2. When misunderstanding between the parties had arisen, as pleaded by the respondent, in 1973 and in May, 1978, the respondent laid the suit for dissolution of the partnership and for accounting etc. It is the respondent's case that the partnership is at will and by issue of notice dissolving the partnership, it stood dissolved with effect from the date of the receipt of the notice by the appellants. He sought to have his share in the partnership ascertained and decree granted accordingly. The appellants contended that under the French Law the partnership is not at will. The contract operates as Law. In terms of the contract Ex. B1 and B2, the respondent has to relinquish his share in favour of the appellants and to take the value thereof without dissolving the firm. One of the issues raised was the maintainability of the suit which was tried as a preliminary issue. Only partnership deeds Ex. B1 and B2 were marked and arguments were addressed on the issue. The Trial Court held that the partnership is not at will. The suit for dissolution of the partnership was not maintainable. The relief of accounting and other remedies were left open. Accordingly the suit was dismissed, which was affirmed, on appeal, by a learned Single Judge.

The Division Bench held that the partnership is at will and the respondent can seek its dissolution. It was further held that the rights of the parties are governed by the Indian Partnership Act 9 of 1932 (for short 'the Act'). The suit was maintainable. Accordingly the appeal was allowed; the suit was restored to file and the Trial Court was directed to try the suit on merits expeditiously.[2]

Held, while allowing the appeal

1. Giving our anxious consideration to the controversy , we have no hesitation to reach the finding and hold that the duration of the partnership has been expressly provided in the deed, namely, that the partnership will continue "till there are two partners" and that, therefore, it is not a partnership at will. Thereby, the respondent has no right to dissolve the partnership except to seek accounting for the period in dispute or his right to withdraw or retire from partnership and to take the value of his share in the partnership either by mutual agreement or at law in terms of the partnership deeds Ex. B-1 and B-2. [18]

2. Though Shri Krishnamurthy Iyer contended that the appellants established a limited company and transferred the assets of the firm to it and thereby the partnership ceased to subsist, we cannot give countenance to the contention for the reason that it is a question of fact and was not raised in the courts below. Therefore, it cannot be raised for the first time in this Court.[19]

3. In case the respondent desires to retire from partnership and the rights and liabilities are not mutually effected, it would be open to the respondent to amend the plaint appropriately and seek a decree in that regard. It is also open to the respondent to seek accounting for the profit during the entire period in dispute as per law. It is also open to the appellants to amend the written statement raising appropriate pleadings, except the limitation. In case the respondent elects to adopt the above course the suit would be disposed of expeditiously giving priority. Otherwise the suit should be dismissed. The appeal is allowed accordingly and we direct the parties to bear their own costs throughout. [20]

Adv. Jayprakash Somani's Videos On Law

Adv. Jayprakash Somani's Videos on Law on Youtube- 'jaysomani64' channel.

1) SLP in Supreme Court / Special Leave Petitions in the Supreme Court of India

2) Transfer of Civil & Criminal Cases by the Supreme Court of India / Transfer of Matrimonial Cases

3) Appellate Jurisdiction of the Supreme Court of India

4) Jurisdictions of the Supreme Court of India

5) Public Interest Litigation in the Supreme Court of India / PIL in Supreme Court

6) Article 32 Writ Petitions in the Supreme Court of India

7) Bail Matters Top 10 Supreme Court Cases

8) FIR Quashing in High Court & Supreme Court

9) Bail & Anticipatory Bail Matters in Supreme Court

10) Insolvency & Bankruptcy Matters in the Supreme Court

11) Insolvency & Bankruptcy Code 2016 Part 1

12) Insolvency & Bankruptcy Code 2016 Part 2

13) Insolvency & Bankruptcy Code 2016 Part 3

14) Corporate Liquidation Process

15) Supreme Court Rules & Procedures Webinar of 2.5 hour on Zoom

16) RDDBFI Act, 1993 (Introduction)

17) The Indian Contact Act 1872

18) Negotiable Instruments Act (Introduction)

19) How to avoid matrimonial disputes& some more videos

20) SEBI Matters in the Supreme Court

21) Matrimonial Matters: Supreme Court's 20 Case Laws

22) Consumer Matters Supreme Court's 20 Case Laws

23) Service Matters Supreme Court's 20 Case Laws

24) How to Search Lawyer for Your Matter

25) Property Matters Supreme Court's 20 Case Laws

26) Bail Matters: Supreme Court's 20 Case Laws

27) Supreme Court / High Court Vacation Benches

28) 69000 Teacher's Recruitment Matters of UP Government in the Supreme Court

29) Contempt of Court Matters in the Supreme Court

30) Advocate Act's Matters in the Supreme Court

31) Business Law Matters in the Supreme Court

32) Banking Matters in the Supreme Court

33) Labour Law Matters in the Supreme Court

34) Arbitration Matters in the Supreme Court

35) Careers in Law -Zoom Webinar by Adv. Jayprakash Somani

36) Civil Matters in the Supreme Court

37) Consumer Protection Act | Consumer Matters in the Supreme Court

38) Corporate Matters in the Supreme Court

39) Criminal Matters in the Supreme Court

40) Role of Respondent in the Supreme Court of India

41) Motor Vehicle Accident Matters in Supreme Court with case laws

42) Article 131 Original Suits in Supreme Court

43) PIL in Supreme Court/ Public Interest Litigations in the Supreme Court of India'

44) CAB Citizenship Amendment Bill is not Unconstitutional

45) Supreme Court of India Cases & Process – Marathi

46) Legal Services Export / Export of Legal Services

47) Transfer of Matrimonial Cases by the Supreme Court of India

48) Public Interest Litigation PIL

49) The Specific Relief Act (Introduction)

50) Corporate Insolvency Resolution Process CIRP

51) ABMM's Career 5 - Careers in Law

52) Transfer of cases by Supreme Court

53) Writ Petitions in High Court & Supreme Court of India

54) Supreme Court Jurisdictions - Appeals, SLP, Writ Petitions, Transfer, Original, Review, Curative

55) LEGAL INDIA TV Show: Cases Handled in Supreme Court

56) Corporate Liquidation Process

57) Legal Services Export / Export of Legal Services

58) Corporate Laws

59) Election Matters- Supreme Court's 20 Case Laws

60) Companies Act, 2013

62) Competition Act, 2002

63) Banking Matters - Supreme Court's 20 Case Laws

64) Election Matters in the Supreme Court

65) Armed Forces Tribunal Matters in the Supreme Court

66) Compassionate Appointment Service matter

67) Foreign Exchange Management Act FEMA

68) Foreign Trade Policy 2021-26 Proposed

69) Customs Act 1962

70) Narcotic Drugs and Psychotropic Substances Act, 1985 NDPS Act

71) Foreign Trade Development & Regulation Act, 1992

72) How to Search Good Advocate in the Supreme Court of India

73) Sr. Adv Vikas Singh's Interview in Nani Palkhivala Wednesday Law Club

74) Indian Penal Code (I. P. C.)

75) Criminal Procedure Code (Cr. P. C.)

76) Commercial Courts & International Arbitration - by Mr. Jaideep Gupta, Senior Advocate in Nani Palkhivala Wednesday Law Club

77) Sr. Adv Ranji Thomos in Nani Palkhivala Wednesday Law Club

78) Urgent Matters in Supreme Court during vacations

79) 498A Bail Matters in Supreme Court

81) 376 Bail Matters in Supreme Court

82) 302, 304, 307, 308 Bail Matters in Supreme Court

83) 138, 420 Bail Matters in Supreme Court

84) POCSO Act Bail Matters in Supreme Court

85) NDPS Act Bail Matters in Supreme Court

86) What is ED (Enforcement Directorate)?

87) Prevention of Money Laundering Act, 2002 (PMLA Act)

88) Insolvency & Bankruptcy Code- Supreme Court Case Laws. Webinar in Nani Palkhivala Wednesday Law Club

89) What is NCLT & NCLAT?

90) Acquittal from 376- Supreme Court's some case laws in Nani Palkhivala Wednesday Law Club dt 28.7.22

91) Insolvency & Bankruptcy in India

92) Can we file case directly in the Supreme Court?

93) Adv. Anuja Pethia has cleared AOR Exam 2021 with 77% marks - Her interview in Nani Palkhivala Wednesday Law Club

94) Customs Act - Supreme Court Case Laws & Interview of AOR Adv. Anuja Pethia in Nani Palkhivala Law Club.

95) The Uttar Pradesh Public Service Tribunals Act, 1976

96) POCSO Act - Supreme Court Case Laws & Interview of AOR Adv. Shoumendu Mukharji & Adv. Nishant Verma in Nani Palkhivala Law Club.

97) Who Can Trigger CIRP Process Under Insolvency Law of India

98) The Uttar Pradesh Government Servant Discipline and Appeal Rules, 1999

99) CIRP Application Under Sec 7 by FC

100) Information Technology Act 2000

101) Uttar Pradesh Recruitment of Dependants of Government Servants Dying in Harness Rules, 1974

102) Foreign Exchange Management Act 1999 & Supreme Court's Case Laws on FEMA & Leading Case of AOR Exam in Nani Palkhivala Law Club.

103) Arbitration and Conciliation Act 1996 & It's Supreme Court Case Laws in Nani Palkhivala Wednesday Law Club.

104) Narcotic Drugs & Psychotropic Substances Act 1985 (NDPS Act) & It's Supreme Court Case Laws in Nani Palkhivala Wednesday Law Club.

105) Recovery of Debts and Bankruptcy Act 1993

106) Uttar Pradesh Land Revenue Code 2006

107) CIRP Application Under Sec 9 by OC

108) CIRP Application Under Sec 10 by CD

109) Hindu Succession Act, 1956

110) Maharashtra Civil Services Rules, 1981

111) Indian Contract Act, 1872 & Supreme Court's Case Laws" in Nani Palkhiwala Wednesday Law Club

112) Securities and Exchange Board of India Act, 1992 i. e. SEBI Act 1992 & Case Laws on Insiders Trading" in Nani Palkhiwala Wednesday Law Club

113) Moratorium Under Section 14 of IBC, 2016

114) Hindu Marriage Act, 1955

115) Maharashtra Land Revenue Code, 1966

116) 64 Leading Cases of AOR Exam Session 1 :- Cases 1 to16 in Nani Palkhiwala Wednesday Law Club

117) 64 Leading Cases of AOR Exam Session 2: Cases 17 to 32 in Nani Palkhiwala Wednesday Law Club

118) 64 Leading Cases of AOR Examination Session 3: Cases 33 to 48 in Nani Palkhivala Wednesday Law Club

119) 64 Leading Cases of AOR Exam Session 4: Cases 49 to 64 in Nani Palkhivala Wednesday Law Club

120) Labour Laws of India: Part 1 - 4 New Labour Law Codes of India

121) New Labour Laws Part 2 The Code on Wages, 2019

122) New Labour Laws Part 3:- The Code on Social Security, 2020

123) Argue in English Fluently & Confidently - Two months online course.

124) SLP Admission in the Supreme Court. 2023 (Hindi)

125) Transfer of Petitions from the Supreme Court (Hindi)

126) Review Petition in the Supreme Court.(Hindi)

127) Recovery of debts from the Company (Hindi)

128) How to search 'Good Insolvency & Bankruptcy Consultant?' (HINDI)

129) Curative Petition in the Supreme Court

130) AFT Appeals in the Supreme Court (HINDI)

131) NCLAT's Appeals in the Supreme Court.

132) Transfer Petition: Which matters can we transfer?

133) SLP Types of SLP in the Supreme court of India (English).

134) Argue in English Fluently and Confidently in the High Court & Supreme Court'.

List Of Adv. Jayprakash Somani's Published Books

1. Supreme Court of India's Leading Case Laws on 'Insolvency & Bankruptcy Code 2016'

2. Bail Matters – Supreme Court's Latest Leading Case Laws

3. Arbitration Matters- Supreme Court's Latest Leading Case Laws

4. Property Matters - Supreme Court's Latest Leading Case Laws

5. Matrimonial Matters- Supreme Court's Latest Leading Case Laws

6. Election Matters- Supreme Court's Latest Leading Case Laws

7. SEBI Matters- Supreme Court's Latest Leading Case Laws

8. Banking Matters- Supreme Court's Latest Leading Case Laws

9. Service Matters- Supreme Court's Latest Leading Case Laws

10. Contempt of Court Matters- Supreme Court's Latest Leading Case Laws

11. Consumer Protection Matters- Supreme Court's Latest Leading Case Laws

12. Corporate Law- Supreme Court's Latest Leading Case Laws

13. Supreme Court's AOR Exam- Leading Cases

14. Armed Force Tribunal - Supreme Court's Latest Leading Case Laws

15. Acquittal From 376 - Supreme Court's Latest Leading Case Laws

16. Negotiable instrument – Supreme Court's Latest Leading Case Laws

17. Contract Act- Supreme Court's Latest Leading Case Laws

18. Insider trading- Supreme Court's Latest Leading Case Laws

19. Foreign Exchange and Management Act- Supreme Court's Latest Leading Case Laws

20. Income Tax Act- Supreme Court's Latest Leading Case Laws

21. Company Law- Supreme Court's Latest Leading Case Laws

22. Competition & Monopoly Matters- Supreme Court's Latest Leading Case Laws

23. Compassionate Appointment- Service Matters- Supreme Court's Latest Leading Case Laws

24. Compulsory Retirement- Service Matters- Supreme Court's Latest Leading Case Laws

25. Voluntary Retirement- Service Matters- Supreme Court's Latest Leading Case Laws

26. Removal/Dismissal/Termination from Service- Supreme Court's Latest Leading Case Laws

27. Seniority- Service Matter- Supreme Court's Latest Leading Case Laws

28. Promotion- Service Matter- Supreme Court's Latest Leading Case Laws

29. Equal Pay for Equal Work- Service Matter- Supreme Court's Latest Leading Case Laws

30. Condition of Service- Service Matter- Supreme Court's Latest Leading Case Laws

31. Customs Act- Supreme Court's Leading Case Laws

32. Information Technology Act- Supreme Court's Leading Case Laws

33. SEC. 125 CR. P. C.- Supreme Court's Leading Case Laws

34. SEC. 498A OF I. P. C.- Supreme Court's Leading Case Laws

35. MOTOR VEHICLE ACT- Supreme Court's Leading Case Laws

36. CONDITION OF SERVICE- SERVICE MATTER- Supreme Court's Leading Case Laws

37. SUSPENSION- SERVICE MATTER- Supreme Court's Leading Case Laws

38. Reservation in SC, ST, OBC- Service Matter- Supreme Court's Leading Case Laws

39. NARCOTIC DRUGS AND PSYCHOTROPIC SUBSTANCES (NDPS) ACT - Supreme Court of India's Latest Leading Case Laws

40. SEC 302 IPC - Supreme Court of India's Latest Leading Case Laws

41. PROTECTION OF CHILDREN FROM SEXUAL OFFENCES ACT (POCSO) - Supreme Court of India's Latest Leading Case Laws

42. PMLA ACT BAIL MATTERS - Supreme Court of India's Leading Case Laws

43. SEC 376 BAIL MATTERS - Supreme Court of India's Leading Case Laws

44. SEC 302 BAIL MATTERS - Supreme Court of India's Leading Case Laws

45. POCSO ACT BAIL MATTERS - Supreme Court of India's Leading Case Laws

46. JUVENILE JUSTICE ACT- Supreme Court of India's Leading Case Laws

47. TRANSFER OF PROPERTY ACT- Supreme Court of India's Leading Case Laws

48. PROFESSIONAL ETHICS OF ADVOCATES- AOR EXAM- SUPREME COURT'S LEADING CASE LAWS

49. WHITE COLLAR CRIME- SUPREME COURT'S LEADING CASE LAWS

50. SEC 302 BAIL MATTERS- SUPREME COURT'S LEADING CASE LAWS

51. SEC 7 IBC 2016 - SUPREME COURT'S LATEST LEADING CASE LAW

52. ADVERSE POSSESSION IN PROPERTY MATTER - SUPREME COURT'S LATEST LEADING CASE LAWS

53. ARMED FORCE TRIBUNAL ACT- SUPREME COURT'S LATEST LEADING CASE LAWs

54. ESSENTIAL COMMODITIES ACT 1955- SUPREME COURT'S LATEST LEADING CASE LAWS

55.'FOREIGN TRADE DEVELOPMENT AND REGULATION ACT'- SUPREME COURT AND HIGH COURT'S LEADING CASE LAWS

Books are available online in India

1. Notion Press: https://notionpress.com/author/jayprakash_somani

2. Amazon: https://www.amazon.in/s?k=jayprakash+somani

3. Flipkart: https://www.flipkart.com/search?q=Jayprakash%20Somani

Books are available online at International Market

4. Amazon International: https://www.amazon.com/s?k=jayprakash+somani

5. Amazon United Kingdom: https://www.amazon.co.uk/s?k=jayprakash+somani

6. E-Books/Kindle edition at National & International Level: https://www.amazon.in/s?k=jaypraksh+somani

Adv Jayprakash Somani's Online Courses

Download our app to get access to our Free Videos, Free Bare Acts, Free Study Material in Legal as well as International Business Regime.

Android App Link ;-https://clpandrea.page.link/cmSm

Ios APp Link :-https://apps.apple.com/us/app/classplus/id1324522260

Login with org code ;- (qywzji)

Web Link ;-https://qywzji.courses.store/

Download App on Google play store - Type

<u>Jayprakash Somani SupremeCourt</u>

Legal Courses :

1. SLP- Bail Matters- Drafting & Successful Arguing in the Supreme Court.

Description - This Course is helpful to Advocates, Litigants, Law Officers, Law Students, Law Schools, Individual. Course contains 8 Videos + Study Material+ PDF Books. Access to this course is for Two Years. Expected duration of this course is one month only.

Topics : 1. SLP- Bail Matters- Drafting & Successful Arguing in the Supreme Court, **2.** Types of bails, **3.** Laws related to bail matters, **4.** How to read Impugned Order of High Court & frame substantial question of laws, **5.** How to draft excellent SLP, **6.** Searching of citations/ case laws, **7.** How to argue in admission hearings, **8.** How argue in after notice hearing.

Speaker: Jayprakash Bansilal Somani, MBA (Foreign Trade), LL. B. Advocate, Supreme Court of India & IP www.jayprakashsomani.com Call: P. A. 9322188701

2. SLP- Succession Matters- Drafting & Successful Arguing in the Supreme Court.

Description - This Course is helpful to Advocates, Litigants, Law Officers, Law Students, Law Schools, Individual. Course contains 9 Videos + Study Material+ PDF Books. Access to this course is for Two Years. Expected duration of this course is one month only.

Topics :1. SLP- Succession Matters- Drafting & Successful Arguing in the Supreme Court, **2.** Information about Succession Matters, **3.** Laws related to Succession Matters, **4.** How to read Impugned Order of High Court to frame substantial questions of law, **5.** How to draft excellent synopsis & list of date, **6.** Drafting of SLP of Succession Matter, **7.** Searching of citations/ case laws, **8.** How to prepare notes & then argue in admission hearings, **9.** How to prepare notes & then argue in after notice final hearing.

Speaker: Jayprakash Bansilal Somani, MBA (Foreign Trade), LL. B. Advocate, Supreme Court of India & IP www.jayprakashsomani.com Call: P. A. 9322188701

3. Legal Vocabulary & its practice pattern to Argue in High Court and Supreme Court / Improve Your Legal English

Description - This Course is helpful to Advocates, Litigants, Law Officers, Law Students, Law Schools, Individual. Course contains 11 Videos + Study Material+ PDF Books. Access to this course is for Two Years. Expected duration of this course is three month only.

Topics : 1. Legal Vocabulary & its practice pattern to Argue in High Court and Supreme Court / Improve Your Legal English, **2.** 1000 legal verbs with its three forms, **3.** Twelve Tenses with its running practice, **4.** One Pdf book on legal vocabulary & its practice pattern with Latin Terms, **5.** Second Pdf book on legal vocabulary & its practice pattern with Latin Terms, **6.** Some Videos of CJI Dr. Dhananjay Chandrachud for the practice of good legal English, **7.** Some Video/Audio Lectures of Legend Nani Palkhivala for standard perfect legal English & flow of Speech, **8.** Some Videos of renowned Sr. Advocates from Mumbai for flow, legal vocabulary & their struggle in legal journey, **9.** Some Videos of Sr. Advocates of the Supreme Court for flow & legal vocabulary, **10.** Some Videos of foreign persons to improve Professional English & thinking process in English, **11.**

Some important legal doctrines with case laws.

Speaker: Jayprakash Bansilal Somani, MBA (Foreign Trade), LL. B. Advocate, Supreme Court of India & IP www.jayprakashsomani.com Call: P. A. 9322188701.

4. SLP- Property Matters - Drafting and Successful Arguing in the Supreme Court.

Description - This Course is helpful to Advocates, Litigants, Law Officers, Law Students, Law Schools 8 Individual. Course contains 9 Videos + Study Material+ PDF Books. Access to this course is for Two Years. Expected duration of this course is one month only.

Topics : 1. SLP- Property Matters - Drafting and Successful Arguing in the Supreme Court, **2.** Types of Property Matters, **3.** Laws related to Property Matters, **4.** How to read Impugned Order of High Court to guide client & frame substantial question of laws, **5.** How to draft Synopsis & List of Dates in Property Matter, **6.** How to draft excellent SLP of Property Matter, **7.** Searching of citations/ case laws with specific paras, **8.** How to argue confidently in admission hearings, **9.** How argue confidently in after notice & final hearings.

Speaker: Jayprakash Bansilal Somani, MBA (Foreign Trade), LL. B. Advocate, Supreme Court of India & IP www.jayprakashsomani.com Call: P. A. 9322188701.

International Business Courses -

1. Agri Products Exports - Scope from India.

Description - This Course is helpful to Agriculturalists, Entrepreneurs, Exporters, Importers, Students. Course contains 12 Videos + Study Material+ PDF Books. Access to this course is for Two Years. Expected duration of this course is one month only.

Topics : **1-** Agri Products Exports - Scope from India, **2.** Agri Export's share in India's total export, **3.** Agri Export Promotional Council's Support, **4.** Top 10 Agri export countries, **5.** Top 10 Agri export product, **6.** India's share in World's Agri Exports, **7.** Onion Exports from India, **8.** Rice Exports from India, **9.** Mango Exports from India, **10.** Fresh Vegetable Exports, **11.** Fresh Fruits Exports, **12.** Export of Agri Allied Products.

Speaker: Jayprakash Bansilal Somani, MBA (Foreign Trade), LL. B. Advocate, Supreme Court of India & IP www.jayprakashsomani.com Call: P. A. 9322188701.

2. Textile Exports - Scope from India.

Description - This Course is helpful to Textile Business Houses, Entrepreneurs, Exporters, Importers, Students. Course contains 14 Videos + Study Material+ PDF Books. Access to this course is for Two Years. Expected duration of this course is one month only.

Topics : 1- Textile Exports - Scope from India, **2.** Textile Export's share in India's total exports, **3.** Support of Textile Export Promotional Council, **4.** Top 10 Countries in Textile Exports, **5.** Top 10 Products in Textile Exports, **6.** Export of Readymade Garments, **7.** Export of Man-made Textiles, **8.** Export of Handloom Products, **9.** Export of Wool & Woollen Textiles, **10.** Export of Silk, **11.** Exports of Handicrafts & Carpets, **12.** Exports of Coir & Coir Manufacturers, **13.** Exports of Jute,14. India's share in World's total textile expor.

Speaker: Jayprakash Bansilal Somani, MBA (Foreign Trade), LL. B. Advocate, Supreme Court of India & IP www.jayprakashsomani.com Call: P. A. 9322188701.

3. Export Import Procedure -Perfect Documentation & It's Management.

Description -This Course is helpful to Business Men, Service Providers, Entrepreneurs, Exporters, Importers, Students. Course contains 13 Videos + Study Material+ PDF Books. Access to this course is for Two Years. Expected duration of this course is three months only.

Topics : **1.** Export Import Procedure, Perfect Documentation & Its management, **2.** Company Formation, **3.** Opening of Bank Account in AD Bank, **4.** Export Procedure points, **5.** Import Procedure Points, **6.** Taking Import Export Code, **7.** Taking RCMC number, **8.** Registration at Port when necessary, **9.** Quality Inspection Certificate of Goods, **10.** CHA & its roll, **11.** Custom Formalities, **12.** Export Documents such as Invoice, Bill of Lading, Insurance Certificate, Quality Inspection Certificate & others, **13.** Excellent Management of Export & Imports Documents.

Speaker: Jayprakash Bansilal Somani, MBA (Foreign Trade), LL. B. Advocate, Supreme Court of India & IP www.jayprakashsomani.com Call: P. A. 9322188701.

4. Jewellery Exports -Scope from India

Description - You can understand world wide scope for Jems & Jewellery in multidimensional ways. 14 videos of this course will create positive spark among you to enter into the Exports & Imports of Gems & Jewellery and other products. Chance to ask your query to Somani Sir every week.

Topics :1. Jewellery Exports - Scope from India, **2.** Jewellery Export's share in India's total exports, **3.** Support of Jems & Jewellery Export Promotional Council, **4.** Top 10 Countries in Jewellery Exports, **5.** Top 10 Products in Jewellery Exports, **6.** Export of Cut & Polished Diamonds, **7.** Export of Gold Jewellery, **8.** Export of Plain Gold Jewellery, **9.** Export of Studded Gold Jewellery, **10.** Export of Silver Jewellery, **11.** Exports of Platinum Jewellery, **12.** Exports of Imitation Jewellery, **13.** Exports of Articles of Gold, Silver & others, **14.** India's share in World's total Jewellery export.

Speaker: Jayprakash Bansilal Somani, MBA (Foreign Trade), LL. B. Advocate, Supreme Court of India & IP www.jayprakashsomani.com Call: P. A. 9322188701.

5. Export Import Finance Management with LC, ECGC & Venture Capital.

Description -You can understand A to Z about International Finance with LC, ECGC & Venture Capital in simple language & with illustrations. 11 videos of this course will create positive spark among you regarding International Finance Management with practical tips. Chance to ask your query to Somani Sir every week.

Topics : 1. Export Import Finance Management with LC, ECGC & Venture Capital, **2.** Which is good & excellent source of finance, **3.** Banking Finance, **4.** List of Banks which provides finance for International Business, **5.** How to start business in Less or Zero Capital, **6.** Letter of Credit, **7.** Types of LCs **8.** Scrutiny of L/C, **9.** ECGC Policy, **10.** Venture Capital Finance., **11.** Ideal formula of Investment & continues growth.

Speaker: Jayprakash Bansilal Somani, MBA (Foreign Trade), LL. B. Advocate, Supreme Court of India & IP www.jayprakashsomani.com Call: P. A. 9322188701.

6. Shipping & Logistics in International Business with live links of Ports, ICDs, CHAs etc.

Description - This Course is helpful to any Businessman, Professionals, Entrepreneurs, Exporters, Importers, CHAs, & Students.

Course contains following 10 Videos + Study Material+ PDF Books. Access to this course is for Two Years. Expected duration of this course is three months only.

Topics : 1. Shipping & Logistics in International Business with live links of Ports, ICDs, CHAs etc, **2.** Roll of CHA in Shipping & Logistics of International Business, **3.** How to find good & genuine CHA, **4.** Courier/

post service for small parcel, **5.** India's important Ports & ICDs with live links, **6.** How & what to study Ports/ ICDs websites, **7.** Art to reduce charges of Shipping & logistics, **8.** Information about some Top International Ports with live links, **9.** Roll of Customs in Exports & Imports,**10.** How to become CHA .

Speaker: Jayprakash Bansilal Somani, MBA (Foreign Trade), LL. B. Advocate, Supreme Court of India & IP www.jayprakashsomani.com Call: P. A. 9322188701.

7. International Business Marketing Part 1: Finding Potential & Genuine Buyers for Exports and Suppliers for Imports.

Description -You can understand Seven Excellent ways to Find Potential & Genuine Buyers for Exports and Suppliers for Imports with illustrations. 11 videos of this course will create positive spark among you regarding International Business Marketing with practical tips. Chance to ask your query to Somani Sir every week.

Topics : 1. International Business Marketing Part 1: Finding Potential & Genuine Buyers for Exports and Suppliers for Imports,**2.** Seven Excellent Ways to find Potential Buyers for Exports, **3.** Top 20 B to B Websites in the World, **4.** Searching Potential Buyers from B to B Sites. Is this safe & good way to search potential buyers, **5.** Searching Potential Buyers through Export Promotional Councils & Its Magazines, **6.** Searching Potential Buyers with help from Embassies, **7.** Searching Potential Buyers through Chamber of Commerce at global level, **8.** Searching Potential Buyers from International Trade Fairs & Exhibitions, **9.** Searching Potential Buyers through your friends & relatives or any Indian Person in focus countries, **10.** How to find focus countries for your products or services, **11.** Taking references from establish buyer/seller.

Speaker: Jayprakash Bansilal Somani, MBA (Foreign Trade), LL. B. Advocate, Supreme Court of India & IP www.jayprakashsomani.com Call: P. A. 9322188701.

8. International Business Marketing Part 2: Communication Skill to take repeated orders from Potential Buyers

Description - You can learn Perfect Communication Skills to initiate International Trade with foreign buyers and art to take repeated orders from these Potential Buyers with illustrations. 11 videos of this course will create positive spark among you to reach upto One Star Exporter Level rapidly and subsequent journey to reach upto Five Star Export House. Chance to ask your query to Somani Sir every week.

Topics :1. International Business Marketing Part 2: Communication Skill to take repeated orders from Potential Buyers,**2.** Preparation of Impressive Company Profile, **3.** Excellent Product CatLog for International Market, **4.** Phone Calls with maintaining dignity of ourself & our country, **5.** Sending emails, **6.** Sending what's app messages, **7.** Technique of repeated follow up, **8.** Art of taking 100% advance payments, **9.** Before giving credit facility how to look credibility of potential buyers or suppliers, **10.** Art of earning good profit of margin, **11.** Art of managing international clients.

Speaker: Jayprakash Bansilal Somani, MBA (Foreign Trade), LL. B. Advocate, Supreme Court of India & IP www.jayprakashsomani.com Call: P. A. 9322188701.